Dr David Owen is Leader of the Social Democratic Party and has been a Member of Parliament for Plymouth since 1966.

He was born in 1938 in Plymouth and educated at Bradfield College; Sidney Sussex College, Cambridge; and St Thomas's Hospital, London, where he qualified as a Doctor of Medicine in 1962. He was Neurological and Psychiatric Registrar from 1964 to 1966 and Research Fellow in the Medical Unit from 1966 to 1968. After his election to Parliament as a Labour Member for the Sutton Division of Plymouth in 1966, he became Parliamentary Private Secretary to the Minister of Defence, Administration. From 1968 to 1970 he was Parliamentary Under Secretary of State for Defence (Royal Navy). When Labour went into Opposition in 1970 he became a front-bench spokesman on defence until his resignation in 1972 over Labour's opposition to Britain's membership of the European Community. Since the General Election of February 1974, following boundary changes, he has represented Plymouth Devonport.

He was Minister of State with responsibility for health in the Department of Health and Social Security from 1974 to 1976. He was created a Privy Councillor in June 1976 and in September became Minister of State at the Foreign and Commonwealth Office. He was appointed Secretary of State for Foreign and Commonwealth Affairs in February 1977, retaining this post until the General Election in May 1979. Thereafter he was Labour Opposition spokesman on energy until 1980.

Dr Owen was one of the founders of the Social Democratic Party, launched in March 1981. He was Leader of the SDP Parliamentary Committee from 1981 to 1982; Deputy Leader from 1982 to 1983; and became Leader of the Party in June 1983.

He has been a member of the Independent Commission on Disarmament and Security Issues since 1980 and a member of the Independent Commission on International Humanitarian Issues since 1983.

Dr Owen is the editor of *A Unified Health Service* (1968) and a contributor to *Social Services for All* (1968). He is also the author of *The Politics of Defence* (1972), *In Sickness and In Health – The Politics of Medicine* (1976), *Human Rights* (1978), and *Face the Future* (1981). He has published articles in the *Lancet, Neurology* and *Clinical Science*.

His wife Deborah is a literary agent. They have two sons and a daughter.

David Owen

A FUTURE
THAT WILL WORK

Competitiveness and Compassion

PENGUIN BOOKS

Penguin Books Ltd, Harmondsworth, Middlesex, England
Viking Penguin Inc., 40 West 23rd Street, New York, New York 10010, U.S.A.
Penguin Books Australia Ltd, Ringwood, Victoria, Australia
Penguin Books Canada Ltd, 2801 John Street, Markham, Ontario, Canada L3R 1B4
Penguin Books (N.Z.) Ltd, 182–190 Wairau Road, Auckland 10, New Zealand

First published 1984
Published simultaneously by Viking

Made and printed in Great Britain by
Richard Clay (The Chaucer Press) Ltd,
Bungay, Suffolk
Filmset in Monophoto Photina by
Northumberland Press Ltd, Gateshead

CONTENTS

PREFACE

This book is entirely based on speeches and articles written in my first year as Leader of the SDP. It is not intended to cover comprehensively all the problems that face Britain today. Some of the ideas have still to be discussed within the SDP and so are not formal policy commitments of the party. Nevertheless I thought it might be helpful to bring together a range of ideas and policies in the hope that it will stimulate debate amongst a wider cross-section of people about the sort of Britain they want to see emerge in the 1990s. I hope the reader will forgive some of the rhetoric and repetition which is a feature of the spoken word, but it seemed better to keep the flavour at times of the political campaigning trail rather than attempt to make the book a dispassionate analysis of Britain in the 1980s and beyond.

ACKNOWLEDGEMENTS

Though responsibility for everything in the book is mine, the speeches, articles and finally the book itself could never have been written without the help of many people too numerous to mention. But particular thanks are due to Maggie Smart, Alex de Mont, Sandra Brenner, Michael Stewart, Barbara Rennie, Harold Carter, Sarah Marks, Tom Burke, Wendy Buckley, Christopher Smallwood, Sue Robertson, Tom McNally, Sarah Horack, Nicholas Bosanquet, Roger Carroll and Hugo Dixon.

Chapter 1 is an expansion of an article first published in *Economic Affairs*, The Longman Group, October 1983; Chapters 3 and 6 contain material first published in *Democracy Must Work*, New York University Press, 1984; Chapter 10 is based on an article first published in *The Political Quarterly*, The Political Quarterly Publishing Co. Ltd, January 1984.

The Social Market Approach

> The Social Democratic idea ... is an obstinate will to erode by inches the conditions which produce avoidable suffering, oppression, hunger, wars, racial and national hatred, insatiable greed and vindictive envy.
>
> Leszek Kolakowski, *Encounter*, February 1982

Britain's economic and industrial problems are deep-seated. To revive our prosperity will require flair, drive and a major shift in attitudes within our economic and industrial life. Though there have been some flickers of improvement in recent export performance, some necessary slimming in the size of some industries' labour forces and increased awareness of the need to compete internationally, we are still not keeping our unit costs sufficiently competitive. Poor productivity in comparison with other countries has been a major factor contributing to our economic difficulties. The British economy is strongly influenced by the state of the world economy, but this must not become an excuse for avoiding problems which are of our own making.

The origins of our economic decline lie deep in the British political and social system. Many of our managers and workers do not trust each other; neither do they cooperate effectively to develop a commercially orientated social climate within industry. Unless these underlying failings can be tackled, our relative economic decline will continue.

Britain cannot recover its economic strength without a far stronger emphasis on winning markets and without a clearer recognition of the commercial and competitive imperatives on which our prosperity depends. It also requires a tougher stance in giving priority to our export industries – ensuring that they do not carry costs greater than their competitors and that the European Community uses its communal strength to enforce genuine free trade.

In Britain, the mixed economy has become a portmanteau description to which virtually anyone can subscribe. An adherent of Clause IV of the Labour Party's constitution invokes the mixed economy, but without any real commitment to the merits of the private sector and without conceding that a market economy is founded on a readiness to take risks which can also bring high rewards. A free-enterprise Conservative Party zealot can espouse the mixed economy without seeing a useful role for government in any part of the economy. The term 'social market' could become a more accurate description of what many see as the correct mixture within the mixed economy. It has been misused on the right by some Conservatives to mean non-interventionism combined with support for the welfare state. It is nevertheless worth re-examining the term, for it could convey the essentials of the Social Democratic approach better than the term 'managed market'. It is a term particularly associated with the 1959 Bad Godesberg programme of the German Social Democratic Party, when the German Social Democrats abandoned Marxist economics and achieved electoral success with thirteen years of a Social Democratic/Liberal coalition government. In Britain, the SDP, founded in 1981, is not a latter-day advocate of laisser-faire, but we do not believe either that market disciplines can or should be avoided. In Britain the economy has developed not simply as a mix between public and private owner-ship but as a mixing of objectives and management attitudes within each sector. There has been a tendency to amalgamate the public and private sectors as part of an amorphous mixed economy rather than to define the frontiers and objectives of the market. There are advantages in keeping the two sectors separate and admitting that one of the necessary differences between them is that profits are the motive force of the private sector and service the motive force of the public sector. The public sector should also, for greater clarity in defining objectives, be broken down further so as to identify the commercial public sector and the public service sector.

In advocating greater decentralization one must recognize that decentralization is not just about us all having more say in the decisions that affect our lives, but about actually making more decisions about our own lives. A decentralized society is one that places a higher priority on choice and diversity than a centralized society does. It leads to smaller units of decision-making, whether in the public or private sector. A movement towards decentralization must by its very nature be an endorsement of the market mechanism. Decentralization challenges the concentration of industrial and economic power that is the legacy of decades of central direction; it also makes one analyse more critically what exactly is meant by the mixed economy.

Socialist revisionists in Britain advocate the mixed economy but refuse to face the political difficulties of admitting that there are necessarily differences between the two sectors. The way to develop the wider social obligations of our commercial managers is to increase their accountability to their own workforce through industrial democracy, profit-sharing, co-ownership and co-operatives, and thus their responsibility to the consumers through competition and fair-trading legislation within these parameters – maximizing profits and re-investing them to provide the dynamics for economic activity. The dwindling democratic socialist wing within the Labour Party has contributed to the emasculation of the private sector by constraining, through regulation, its driving force – profits. It has appeared not to understand that by weakening the private sector's scope for initiative, aggressiveness and boldness, its economic performance is fatally sapped. It has also frequently undermined the public service sector by forcing it to ape the private sector unnaturally, concentrating on rather bogus profit accounting and giving the impression that service to the public is no longer to be the mainspring of its activity.

The non-profit-making public service sector requires different management techniques, yardsticks of efficiency and strategic objectives from those adopted for the commercial public sector, which must accept and live by market disciplines. In government, one of the skills of influencing the national economy is to understand the extent to which an amalgamation of public and private sector attitudes and policies destroys the dynamics of the systems – when curbing profits limits investment, when squeezing prices limits expansion, when interference in wage-bargaining affects productivity, when job security impairs innovation and risk-taking. The economy needs to operate within a flexible framework that allows for swift responses to changes in world markets.

There are many signs that the existing framework of the mixed economy is too rigid and too unresponsive, and that Britain is stultified by inbuilt resistance to change. Further, our ability to adjust to and to anticipate changes in world markets is lamentable compared with that of our major competitors. The response to this of the Conservative government has been to embark on an extensive programme of privatization. In some areas this has proved to have some merit, but it has little value where a state-owned monopoly is merely turned into a privately owned monopoly and where competition in the market is reduced rather than increased. It is not only the public sector in Britain that is authoritarian, timid and unimaginative. Many of these failings are deeply entrenched in large private companies. Privatization does not of itself produce changes of attitude in the management of a particular firm, nor on the shop floor. Yet the changing of attitudes is crucial.

The British government should promote change in attitudes at the periphery, not solely at the centre. We need to give as much attention to micro-economic policy as to macro-economic policy and to create in Britain a genuinely social market economy. This means accepting a more restrained view of the role of government and giving more attention to the value of marginal change. It means a less doctrinaire and ideological approach to industry. It means introducing industrial democracy as a vital reform that needs a legislative impetus but cannot be rigidly imposed. It is an approach that is searching for the correct balance between decisiveness and participation, and favours organic growth from within an organization. The essence of the social market approach is that no economic or industrial policy can be introduced by central government diktat without considerable distortion of other policies.

The present Conservative government has been as deeply centralist as its predecessors. The number of mergers has soared, the Monopolies Commission recommendations have been overridden, the regulatory power of central government in many areas has increased at the expense of both private and public industry. It is odd that a supposedly free-market government has spawned an OFTEL superstructure for the telecommunications market, a regulatory body for cable TV and satellite broadcasting recommended by a committee under the chairmanship of a former Secretary to the Cabinet, and has merged the Trade and Industry Departments rather than creating a small Ministry for Competition to bust open private and public cartels and monopolies. Such a Ministry would also be responsible for demerging large private corporations and curtailing any market abuse by the multinationals, and would disaggregate the public sector as part of a strategy which would include privatization only where it could be shown to promote greater competition in the market and a wider ownership of capital.

Clarifying the different roles and techniques of managing and controlling the commercial market-dominated sector and the public service sector is the essential prelude to achieving stronger coherence and the right balance for the national economy. Coherence also demands a reluctance to implement structural industrial changes which appear to have no long-term hope of being accepted by other parties and are virtually certain to be reversed if the government changes. This is not intended to exclude the imposing of structural changes which are politically controversial – it is to argue that far higher priority should be given, when making industrial changes, to ensuring that they have a reasonable chance of lasting.

For some, on both the right and the left, such an approach is an impossible discipline to accept. They depict it as a prescription for 'middle-of-the-road' consensus politics. Why, they say, are the same arguments not applied to education, health and social policy? In the areas of social policy in post-war Britain there has been in fact far more continuity between governments than there has been in economic or industrial policy. Yet it is our economic and industrial success which determines the national wealth, which alone can support, extend and improve our education, health and social services.

We cannot continue ill-judged political experiments with British industry, whether through dogmatic non-intervention by the state or by widespread interventionist, statist policies. Britain's industrial base is crumbling, and far faster than in other comparable countries. The best way of checking the ideological zealotry of British politics in industrial matters, as in others, is to introduce proportional representation. Not surprisingly the appeal of electoral reform is gaining ground in industry and commerce, where the 'strong-government' argument beloved by politicians and journalists carries less conviction when contrasted with industry's experience of the disruption and uncertainty accompanying the ideological switchback of alternating Labour and Conservative governments.

The social market approach to the economy does not advocate retaining the status quo. It does not accept current levels of unemployment, nor does it tolerate present inequalities. The message is necessarily complex, for it believes that there is no magic formula or single initiative that will miraculously set Britain back on the road to recovery, and that those politicians who pretend otherwise are guilty of perpetuating a cruel misconception.

The social market advocates openly some form of incomes policy because it recognizes that the dilemma is how to pursue a more expansionary policy designed to reduce unemployment without triggering inflation. It recognizes that in the private sector, market realism on wage-bargaining cannot be guaranteed at a time of expansion. There has been over the last few years in Britain a welcome return to sanity over wage-bargaining and many negotiations have been rooted in what the particular employer can afford. But how much this new-found realism owes to a continued fear of unemployment remains to be seen. It has also been accompanied by a loss of industrial production and jobs far in excess of what was necessary. One cannot be sure that running the British economy at a higher level of activity than at present would not trigger inflation; hence the need to develop a viable incomes policy ready to use if necessary. Similarly, anticipating the situation when the economy recovers means establishing now the framework for a genuine understanding by individual workforces of their firm's economic and market position, its profit forecasts, its investment plans, its hopes for productivity, its employment potential. In this context, industrial democracy is not a fringe issue for British industry but an essential reform. The works-council and co-determination laws in West Germany have contributed to the far greater awareness, by their trade unionists, of commercial realities, of the importance of maintaining existing markets and of winning new orders. These laws have also contributed to their better managerial record and relations with the shop floor. Increased democracy within trade unions and in workplace management is also the only socially acceptable way of providing the framework for tempering social aspirations with market realities.

Against such a background, when the competition for labour increases as economic activity picks up, wage-bargaining need not in the short term induce the inflationary stimulus of the past, and more jobs could be created on the basis of a non-inflationary expansion. The problem is, however, that a considerable part of the private sector does not at present operate in a real market. Tougher controls over monopoly power and more emphasis on trust-busting will take time to establish and take effect. What can be done in the meantime? Experience tells us that if market realism is to be maintained in the long term over wage-bargaining in the private sector and the commercial public sector, it will not be done by reviving the centralized prices-and-incomes policies of the past, with their fixed norms or percentages and unselective 'fairness' compressing differentials and creating endless anomalies. These policies not only failed to redistribute income; they also failed to limit inflation in the longer term. They were fatally flawed in that their centralized nature did not allow unions and employers to negotiate within the framework of profit and productivity that related to the specific firm. They took little account of the rapid decentralization of wage-bargaining in Britain and the extent to which, as the Donovan Commission noted in 1968, decision-making had moved downwards from the national trade union officers to committees of shop stewards.

The national economy needs a decentralized and flexible incomes strategy, ideally with the bargaining covering employment, pensions and working hours as well as pay, all related as closely as possible to day-to-day working practice and not susceptible to a national formula. A more decentralized pattern of negotiating cannot, however, be quickly or easily achieved. Old habits die hard; the present decision-makers in government and in industry all tend to be centralists and will not easily give up their grip on the negotiations. A key question is whether trade unionists and managers in the regions and in the workplace even want to accept responsibility. We should be looking hard at the more widespread use of arbitration, with both sides voluntarily making contractual agreements for fixed periods; these could then be made legally binding later on. Arbitration should be extended to cover job security agreements. There is also merit in pendular, or final-offer, arbitration, where the arbitrator can only choose either the employer or the employees' case, and is not empowered to split the difference. This makes for hard-headed negotiating in which differences are minimized, whereas splitting-the-difference arbitration maximizes disagreement and is invariably in-flationary.

All these changes, and the introduction of industrial democracy at the workplace rather than at the centre, will make it easier to achieve non-inflationary, decentralized wage-bargaining and take job security into account. The problem is most acute in the short term, particularly if the rise in unemployment is to be checked.

In order to guard against inflation being fuelled by a measure of reflation, we must consider mechanisms for achieving income restraint and prepare statutory powers for use in the last resort. The first objective should involve an openly stated annual forward estimate of the percentage range within which negotiations should take place, to be arrived at after discussions between management, unions and government. The government would have to keep within this range for their public sector employees. This would allow for a varied non-inflationary pattern of wage settlements within the agreed percentage range for the private sector. It is prudent for government to anticipate a situation when private sector wage-negotiating may become inflationary and to prepare for this eventuality by putting on the statute books an inflation tax as a reserve power. The successful firm that wished to pay above the pay range could avoid paying inflation tax by distributing the excess in shares to its employees and, provided the shares were not marketable for some years, it would not fuel inflationary pressures. Powers to investigate monopoly price rises would be required when the cost appeared to be being passed on in inflationary pay settlements.

These are negative measures, and it should not be necessary to implement them. Yet experience shows that a viable though flexible incomes strategy would be far more likely to be negotiated if all concerned were under no illusion that, without some agreement, government would not shirk from declaring, on its own responsibility, a range within which incomes should be negotiated and introducing an inflation tax to uphold that policy. The main task of any incomes strategy is to ensure that money GDP (Gross Domestic Product) in the economy can be increased and sustained, more people can be employed and the private and public sectors can operate efficiently. Voluntary agreement would be much easier to achieve in a more buoyant economy, where unemployment was at least moving down as a result of a gradual expansion, with only a limited effect on inflation. In Britain, with high unemployment bound to continue for some years, there is the basis for a deal where unions, management and government offer respectively incomes restraint, increased investment and a higher level of economic activity.

The hardest partner to convince of the necessity of making a deal in the interim, so that one can establish a system of non-inflationary comparability that will last, will be the public service sector. Here the unions are strong, covering some 80 per cent of the employees. Most post-war strikes have taken place in this sector and with the nationalization and centralization that occurred during and after the Second World War the unions know that the potential disruption from nationwide strike action is considerable. In some areas of the public service there is little scope for the productivity dealing that exists in the commercial sector and which can ease the restrictiveness of wage restraint. In the past, the public service sector unions, particularly when demand for labour was high, were able to bargain nationally for higher wages while maintaining virtual job security. Recently, however, job security has been lost and demand for labour is low. What is needed is the sort of non-inflationary pay comparability system that is discussed in Chapter 3.

Judging by opinion surveys, the public mood in relation to public services is ambivalent. People want high standards of service and, whether in public health or education, can be persuaded that they should in theory pay for them. But when it comes to actually paying higher charges, rates or taxes, there is a resistance that appears to go beyond the natural reluctance to pay out. It is an open question whether this resistance would be less if standards were perceived to be improving or at least being maintained. Falling standards are not the best way of encouraging people to accept that they must pay more for these public services. Another difficulty is that the public, rightly or wrongly, feels that their requirements as consumers are often ignored by an insensitive public service bureaucracy. Yet the public frequently demands the regulation and accountability that breeds the bureaucracy they dislike. These ambivalent feelings are now running too deep to be ignored by the public sector unions, their management or the government.

Either the monopoly bargaining power of the public sector unions will have to be curbed and efficiency audits, with the cessation of fixed tenure for senior management, introduced within the existing structure, or the structure itself will be changed by public demand.

In public services where the revenue is raised through charges – telephones, post, gas, electricity, rail, water – the monopoly cannot easily be broken. If the unions will not accept agreement covering comparability, arbitration and no-strike provision, smaller autonomous managerial units, more cooperatives and the widespread use of franchising will become inevitable. But dis-aggregation of national wage-bargaining procedures will only help if there is a decentralized employing authority with the ability to fix prices and wages. There is already a case for autonomous all-purpose regional electricity authorities for England, as in Scotland, for regional autonomy for the gas industry and, perhaps more controversially, the railways.

Franchising could be a very attractive solution, for it provides a way of enabling enterprises to act competitively, but within a framework which protects the public interest in a way which entirely unregulated competition would not. The private provision of hitherto publicly provided goods and services, subject to official, contractual, licensing or regulatory requirements, opens up a host of possibilities, even in the natural monopoly areas, as alternatives to nationalization on the one hand or large private monopolies subject to regulatory commissions on the other. Neither of these choices is attractive. Privatization of British Telecom, involving the creation of a private instead of public monopoly, is no progress. But just as the Traffic Commissioners granted bus companies franchises which obliged them to cover social as well as profitable routes, so licences could be granted only to those telecommunications operators who would be prepared to meet social as well as commercial obligations.

One can envisage rival groups running competing regional electricity networks and gas boards, and competing against each other for the franchises. Franchises could be issued for sub-activities within nationalized industries such as the catering facilities on stations or trains – as an alternative to privatization and as a method of providing pressure for improved efficiency while at the same time ensuring the public's needs continue to be met.

Successive governments have undercapitalized the public service sector and have never hesitated to raise charges as a short-term means of acquiring revenue. What these industries require is more freedom over their investment. Where government subsidy is judged necessary, it should be separated out and an attempt made to identify the social return. There is no intrinsic reason why public services should not be subsidized, but blanket subsidy breeds complacency and induces financial indiscipline.

The critical issue for the public services is how to manage them more efficiently and provide a better-quality service. They are frequently too large and, even when broken down into smaller units, operate national wage-bargaining agreements. Regional water authorities with the power to levy different water rates ought to be democratically accountable and bargain locally, not nationally. Local government also negotiates wage rates nationally. It will be difficult to decentralize this process until financial autonomy has been given back to local government and until there is proportional representation of local opinion in the council chamber. There is a genuine fear that if the government introduced local income tax to pay for local government services, replacing rates in their present form, some councils would raise local income tax irresponsibly. Yet local income tax is the best way of phasing out rates, and of relating the quality of local authority services to their financing. Nevertheless it is a tax that must be responsibly handled.

It is amazing that the National Health Service employees' wage-bargaining has become closely linked with local authority wage negotiations. This linkage should be broken. Eventually democratically elected district authorities should be empowered to raise part of their revenue by fixing a health tax as part of local income tax and to negotiate locally. Some will argue that any disaggregation of wage-bargaining will of itself be inflationary, with a ratchet effect as weak local bargaining units set the pace for an upward spiral. But against this it can be argued that a strong, smaller and more responsive bargaining authority can not only check an inflationary spiral but also protect employment in their own area if there is the will to do so from their workforce. There is little evidence that, with the powerful public sector unions, the present system of centralized bargaining has led to lower inflation; on the contrary, the reverse seems to have been the case.

Centralized bargaining has also severely limited the opportunity to trade off wage restraint against job creation or to allow local choice to protect services. In most public services the voice of the consumer is now, in effect, the voice of national government – which is so far removed from the final service that it can readily live with short-term decisions creating adverse long-term consequences or falling standards of service. Arguments about the quality of service will always tend to go by default in a centralized system. Quality arguments will only be able to counter the quantity arguments, which are a natural but vested interest of the public service unions, if there is stronger consumer representation at the bargaining table. Scotland has separate bargaining procedures in many sectors, with wage rates different from those operating in England and Wales. In London there has to be a special public service weighting allowance. In these cases, the principle of national rates has already been significantly breached. There is a strong case for a determined attempt to change existing public service bargaining procedures.

But government cannot just concern itself with bargaining procedures. In all western industrialized democracies, governments of the left and right have adopted, willingly or otherwise, an industrial strategy. No industrial strategy can in practice be operated by any government without regulation or centralized interference in industry. Government should not aim to intervene, however, in an attempt to override market forces, which would only lock the economy into an ossified industrial structure. It should rather aim to anticipate, along with industry, what is likely to be demanded in the marketplace in a few years' time and to accelerate the process of adaptation to those demands by stimulating science, technology and skill training, with the objective of helping to create a successful, competitive economy.

The aim should be to produce the climate for a genuine partnership between government and industry by promoting changes in attitude. A current bestseller, *In Search of Excellence – Lessons from America's Best Run Companies*, demonstrates what we need in Britain. It describes how the companies invested in top quality. They fawned on their customers. They listened to their employees and treated them like adults. They allowed some chaos in return for quick action and regular experimentation. These are the attitudes that should permeate outwards from an industrial strategy, but such attitudes cannot be ordered up by government fiat.

A democratic politician governs by consent; change in attitudes, the importance of which can hardly be exaggerated, takes time to develop. It is not ignoble or foolish to believe that market realities will be accepted more quickly in Britain if government is prepared to accept some responsibility for the legacy of the past rather than putting the whole burden of adjustment, quite unfairly, on the shoulders of those people who happen to be caught up in the process. The necessary economic adjustments, which are promoted by market forces, sometimes need to be phased and cushioned by government intervention if there is not to be great economic waste and social hardship. In the declining industries, any government action should be temporary and be linked to a clear industrial strategy; objectives should include a timed schedule for restructuring, de-manning, retraining and product reorientation. One of the strengths of the EEC is that it curbs the tendency of its member governments to capricious protectionism. It acts slowly, sometimes maddeningly so, but at least it provides a multilateral framework for action in a world where pure free trade has long ceased to be a reality and where an ability to counter repeated and outrageous breaches of fair-trading practices is a necessity, and the only factor restraining even more unilateral and damaging protectionism.

Neither acceptance of bipartisan mercantilism nor a government strategy for the new technology is contrary to the philosophy of a social market economy. The prefix 'social' is not accidental, nor should it be dismissed as irrelevant by the advocates of laisser-faire. We are economically and industrially very weak in a world where protectionism abounds. In order to gain democratic support for accepting market disciplines there has to be some tempering of the social consequences. It is not unreasonable to give Lancashire more time to adjust to the world textile market or to consider what would happen to small farmers and rural communities if there was no intervention over pricing. Nor are voluntary restraint policies reprehensible if they are temporary (though the pressures that develop to make them in effect permanent can be hard to resist).

In the past, much of the pressure for protection has come from industries where Britain has little chance of remaining, or becoming again, internationally competitive. In the long term there are no good industrial-policy arguments for depriving the British consumer of good cheap foreign shoes or video machines in response to special pleading by an industry which wants to be sheltered indefinitely from competition.

International interdependence has become a cliché, but it is a fact of central importance in the economic life of this country. Since the Second World War, the British economy – like that of other western countries – has become progressively more closely integrated with the rest of the world, as a result of specialization, through trade, through flows of capital and, to a lesser extent, through movements of people. Exports account for a third of our GDP. Interdependence imposes limitations on what we can do independently, but it is also beneficial. It is beneficial because of the gains which advanced industrial economies – and for that matter others – derive from competition and specialization. This was why British governments of both parties dismantled wartime restrictions, supported successive rounds of trade liberalization and took us into the EEC. It was the Attlee government, not the Conservatives, who made a bonfire of wartime trade and exchange controls and led the way to Britain's integration into the international economy.

This prompts the question: should we accept and promote international competition as vigorously as we promote domestic competition? Are we genuine free-traders? The answer, even with qualifications, must be yes, though this will not always be a popular answer, since those in the front line of international competition will see foreign goods as a threat. We need to have the courage to point to the wider benefits of open markets – both to exporters and to consumers, who benefit from lower prices and greater choice. And on occasions – European agriculture is the most obvious – we need to take strong issue with pressure groups of protectionist producers.

There are, however, important qualifications which must be made. One is the necessity to give some protection to industries – and services – of the future, the genuine 'infant industries'. Another area where qualification is necessary is where our trading partners break the rules – on 'dumping' for example; in such cases the European Community must be free to act, not least to maintain the support of public opinion for the consequences of freeing our internal market. But Britain must be careful not to allow – under cover of cries of 'unfairness' – foreigners to become scapegoats for the failures produced by our own history of class-ridden industrial relations and complacent economic management. There are cases where international competition must hurt the weak and vulnerable: high unemployment regions; minority groups; low paid workers. For Social Democrats, competition, across as well as within national borders, is necessary and desirable, but it is not sufficient. It must be buttressed by active regional manpower and social policies which help those caught up in painful economic change. The poignancy of this is heightened by the fact that some of the international competition which is most fiercely resisted domestically originates in poor countries.

The moral certainty which used to inspire thinking about development in this country has become somewhat dulled. We have inevitably become preoccupied with our own high unemployment and social ills. The massive disparity between rich and poor countries is given less priority as we acknowledge that within our own society more people are now suffering because of unemployment. Also, some poorer countries are clearly seen to have progressed economically either through rapid industrialization or by oil revenues. A large part of the world's population, however, especially in south Asia and sub-Saharan Africa, is desperately poor. In low-income Africa, per capita incomes, already at subsistence level, actually declined in the 1970s and are now lower than at the beginning of the 1960s. Economic decline and drought mean widespread hunger and malnutrition. The massive pool of the world's destitute, the absolute poor – a total of 800 million was estimated recently – is swelling annually.

Both the social compassion and the market realism of the social market philosophy have a role to play in addressing these problems. It means recognizing a moral obligation that is not discharged through private charity – useful though this may be – any more than domestic poverty and inequality can be tackled without the state playing a central role, through benefits and social services. Hence we accept the importance of overseas aid as a vehicle for resource transfers. The SDP/Liberal Alliance has made a strong commitment in its manifesto to achieving 0.7 per cent of GNP as a target for overseas aid within five years in government and has rejected the arguments of those who oppose both the moral and economic basis for aid.

While the approach to at least the poorest of developing countries must have a strong compassionate element there is an important role for the market too. Aid can provide only part of the capital flows which are required by developing countries if they are to grow; for the middle-income countries of Latin America and the Far East aid will be unimportant. It is necessary for developing countries to be able to help themselves to earn foreign exchange through trade as well as aid.

Many countries rely on commodities and while they can be helped, by compensatory financing arrangements and possibly through buffer stocks, to offset the effects of instability, there is frankly not a great deal which can be done by international action to prevent adverse price trends if there is an excess of supply relative to demand on the world market. To this extent, the ambitious schemes put forward in the 1970s for trying to manage world commodity markets have limited prospects. What the more successful developing countries have done is to diversify their exports into manufactures, services and the processing of raw materials. This has clearly had major implications for our own economy. It is inevitable that more and more developing countries – not just Hong Kong and Korea – will become competitive in these products and cease to play a traditional colonial role as 'hewers of wood and drawers of water'. Of course, this process cannot be one-sided; as the more successful developing countries demand access to our markets, so we are justified in expecting them to remove protective barriers. But one of the most important political tasks in the 1980s and 1990s will be to help the British people to understand and face a world in which adjustments to new sources of competition have to be made. It is a task for which the Labour Party, with its inward-looking approach and hostility to markets, and the Conservative Party, with its instinctive nationalism and lack of sympathy for the poorer half of the world, are equally ill-equipped.

We must also recognize the value of private capital markets in relations between rich and poorer countries. There has been in many parts of the Third World an over-reaction to some of the excesses perpetrated by overseas investors, a tendency – as on the British left – to see multinational companies as part of some international capitalist conspiracy. As a consequence, foreign investment in many developing countries has fallen sharply and they have become over-reliant for overseas capital on bank credit at high interest rates, without the advantages of foreign entrepreneurship, risk-taking and skills. While we must not make the mistake of many on the right of assuming that foreign investment is a form of aid – clearly it benefits the investor as much, if not more, than the recipient – we should not be afraid to defend private investment in poorer countries as much as in our own.

Just as in our own country, so also in many developing countries there is currently a reaction against overcentralized government and badly thought-out government intervention and planning. There is now abundant evidence of the damage done to developing countries by the grosser forms of market distortion: overvalued exchange rates which have dampened exports and encouraged smuggling; artificially low food prices which have discouraged food production and impoverished peasant farmers; minimum wages which have aggravated unemployment; subsidization of petrol which has promoted oil imports. At the same time many of those governments of the right which have sought to rectify these market distortions have – like our own in Britain – done so in a way which is insensitive to the interests of their poorest citizens, and often brutal. The ideas of the social market economy have relevance here as an alternative approach. We should not be embarrassed or discouraged by cries of 'neo-colonialism' from openly identifying with governments in developing countries which are trying, often in extremely adverse circumstances, to combine the pursuit of economic growth and market efficiency with a genuine commitment to the poorest social groups.

We also need to stress the mutuality of interest between our country and developing countries. If the British public is to accept greater flows of aid as a public expression of compassion and freer international markets in pursuit of economic efficiency, they will need to be persuaded that it is in their long-term interest. This enlightened self-interest has two essential components; one, the main theme of the Brandt Report, is that developing countries are potentially an enormous market for the goods and services of our underemployed economy and that they can be helped, through aid and trade measures, to acquire purchasing power in terms of foreign exchange. What they earn, they spend on our goods.

The other aspect of this self-interest is of a less material and less measurable kind – the sense which many of us have, based both on historical experience and on what is now happening in many parts of the developed world, that economic crisis leads to political instability. Political eruptions derive directly from painful economic adjustment. Several of the sub-Saharan African countries are becoming unmanageable because of economic collapse. In some cases this instability can spill over into great power rivalry and conflict. The vast disparity between the escalating outlay in military hardware and the total neglect of preventative peacekeeping through the UN system was highlighted in *Common Security*, the report of the Palme Commission. The Brandt and Palme Commissions met together in 1983 to discuss these interrelated issues. A self-defeating neglect of those unstable parts of the Third World is seen in the drying-up of funds for development agencies such as the World Bank. The western democracies know that assisting poor countries economically can help to head off the social collapse which threatens many of them. But, even so, we do not match our political rhetoric about free societies with economic action to support free societies.

We now face an imminent crisis in the global economy which, while it affects developing countries most seriously, also has major implications for those of us in industrial countries. It has several manifestations: the global slump in world trade and production, only very modestly alleviated by the recovery initiated in the USA; unprecedentedly high levels of real interest rates; a bank debt crisis which has been shelved rather than solved; growing conflict and lack of understanding over trade, exchange rates and economic management between the USA, Japan and Europe.

The dangerous breakdown of the international economy on which we depend has two components, both of which reflect a lack of balance within the economy. Firstly, there is no longer a reasonable balance in international finance. There has been a virtually complete privatization of international credit. It was originally envisaged by Keynes and the founding fathers of the post-war system at Bretton Woods that underpinning the international financial system there would be a strong central authority, a kind of world central bank which would ensure that there was an adequate, well-regulated supply of international liquidity. The IMF has been but a pale shadow of that original dream. In the 1970s it was the private banking system, operating through Eurodollar markets, which met the international demand for credit, especially in the aftermath of the OPEC price explosion. The bankers deserve great credit for having rapidly improvised, through private capital markets, the recycling of OPEC surpluses to deficit countries. But a state of great instability has been created, in which there is a large 'overhang' of commercial debt owed by debtor Third World countries. And there are grave doubts about whether the banks can continue to make available an adequate flow of funds to meet the balance-of-payments deficits of these countries and to help them service their rescheduled debts. A much better balance needs to be struck between public and private responsibilities in the international field to ensure that, at the very least, the International Monetary Fund and the World Bank are given the vitally necessary resources. This is a very dangerous time for the Right in the US, and to a lesser extent in Europe, to be indulging their prejudices about the alleged evils of all forms of government and intergovernment intervention.

The other dimension to the current crisis is the growing lack of cooperation between governments. It is a sad commentary on the competence of the main western governments, which supposedly believe passionately in a free-market system, that they cannot cooperate through GATT to prevent a steady decline in respect for international trading rules and the growth of protectionist sentiment. There is, moreover, an almost complete lack of cooperation between western governments regarding macro-economic management, shown by the failure of the 1984 London economic summit talks. The primitive idea that all that is necessary is for different countries to put their own house in order is painfully contradicted by the effects of US deficit financing on international interest rates; by the erratic and destabilizing movements of exchange rates; and by the way in which slump inflation in major countries is transmitted to others. This approach to economic policy, which blithely ignores the realities of interdependence, is no less dangerous than the idea that Britain should retreat into an inward-looking siege economy. The Left's fetish of nationalization looks very jaded, given its objective record within the post-war British economy. Yet any British government has to decide, as part of its industrial strategy, on the role of the commercial public sector. Is it just a staging-post between public and private ownership, or can it be the vehicle for the imaginative, practical and enthusiastic development of industrial democracy, for share-ownership schemes like that introduced for the National Freight Corporation? Is public ownership just about efficiency and acting commercially, because, if so, privatization will be harder to resist. In a strategy for the new technologies, can the public commercial sector be used imaginatively to move ahead of the private sector and take risks, a policy made possible by the freedom to reinvest more profits rather than distribute them to shareholders looking for income, not capital growth? Would Inmos have ever established itself in Britain without the initial public investment? Would the inventive skills of Sir Clive Sinclair have ever been turned into a commercial success without the vital initial backing of the National Research and Development Corporation (NRDC)? The workers in British Steel, British Leyland, British Airways and British Aerospace have the right to share in the profits and must expect their wages to be held back if there are no profits. Yet, because of international competition, none of these companies has an absolute monopoly; they operate where there is a definable national interest and at least a case for a public as opposed to a purely private viewpoint being represented in their long-term decision-making.

In reality any determined Chancellor of the Exchequer could alter the present absurd public sector accounting conventions at a stroke, given the political will. This would avoid using privatization as a backdoor method of freeing the commercial public sector's investment programme. We should try to end the yo-yo polemics about nationalization or privatization, bring market-orientated disciplines to the commercial public sector, achieve more stability, but we should not freeze the frontier between the public and private sectors. It is best neither to endorse the status quo nor close one's mind to the objective case for privatization but to put the onus of proof on to those who wish to change the frontiers.

This approach also fits naturally with a measure of government planning. The saddest aspect of policy development in Britain has been the decline over the last sixteen years in the politician's confidence in the contribution that planning can make to the development of an industrial strategy. Planning is not concerned merely with building an information base; it also involves anticipating trends and taking action to prevent or mitigate foreseeable adverse social situations. There is no contradiction in putting the case for the social market and further decentralization, and at the same time arguing for more planning. They can logically run in harness. Sensible decision-making implies careful assessment of the right level for making decisions – international, national, regional or local. In a decentralized system it is even more necessary to establish links, so that information and experience are carried back from a wide spread of decision points.

The ghosts of past failure are still strong; the collapse of the 1965 National Plan and the slow dismembering of the Department of Economic Affairs still arouse painful memories. But if the Labour government in 1964 had devalued, and made growth its priority policy, its whole planning initiative might have been a success. The 1974–9 Labour government tried to develop planning through industrial sector working-parties as part of a less ambitious overall industrial strategy developed within the framework of the National Economic Development Organization. Some valuable work was done but the structure, by concentrating on ensuring representation of industrial sectors, tended to encourage a fragmented approach to planning, with a high degree of special pleading. More critically, the ambivalence of the last Labour government over planning agreements and further nationalization undermined confidence in the private sector.

Imaginative policies towards employment planning are more important in the long term than many of the changes relating to industrial structure, for without skilled employees no company, private or public, can compete. Skill training helps to break down class barriers and create a more socially mobile population. It can contribute directly to industrial harmony by educating workers to understand the basis for decisions which affect them and participate more in the decision-making process. The acquisition of skills, especially by those from poor family backgrounds – who are at present the worst served by the education system – can help in reducing social tensions arising from unemployment among ethnic minorities and inner-city youth, and in easing the transition to new technology. This is an area where there is quantifiable economic and social return.

The social market is a philosophy that embraces more than just efficiency and industrial partnership – it also has a commitment to a classless and more equal society, and this cannot be set aside to wait until economic growth is achieved. It is part of the recipe for achieving higher growth in a socially acceptable atmosphere. Society must grapple simultaneously with the values inspired by a competitive market economy and the values to be fostered in a society determined to reduce social deprivation and poverty. An ability to compete does not exclude a sense of injustice or a desire to shoulder some of the burden of alleviating poverty. Altruism can exist in the hearts of export managers as well as social workers.

Successive governments have failed to grapple effectively with the poverty in our midst because they have not motivated the spirit of altruism or fraternity in society. The system of welfare benefits is a maze and a mess. A priority for the next decade is not only to create more incentives for executives, but also, more importantly, to remove the disincentives at the lower scales of income. There is at present a surtax on poverty. Not only is help for poor people grossly inadequate in amount; it is also totally inadequate in its coverage. To tackle these points at the roots we have to raise the real value of benefits generously and to simplify the whole system.

This can be done only by adopting a policy of selectivity and abandoning universality as the overriding welfare principle.

This selective approach is crucial. Unless help is focused on the most needy, scarce resources will be wasted and we will fail to alleviate poverty. To wait for some future economic recovery before attacking poverty carries no guarantee that it will be done even then. Though in theory redistribution is easier at times of faster economic growth, experience shows that the attitudes and values that prevail during the few periods of rapid growth too often seem peculiarly prone to a selfish, never-had-it-so-good outlook. The task is to foster the spirit of generosity and harness it to provide help for those in need. That generous spirit has been stultified by the bureaucracy and red tape of our social security system. It has also been dampened by the feeling, widespread among average earners, that the incentive to work is insufficient and the gap between take-home pay and the dole money too narrow.

These matters must be of concern to us all and we cannot reverse our relative economic decline by arguing whether competitiveness should take second place to compassion or compassion second place to competitiveness. We need them both. The point is discussed further in Chapter 7.

Without a social conscience to modify commercial realism, the polarization of British society will continue and the disadvantaged in society will feel increasingly alienated. We need partnership in politics as well as in industry. Unemployment shows every sign of remaining stubbornly high. The challenge for the 1990s is to find ways of encouraging early retirement, an end to regular overtime, a move towards a shorter working week and the introduction of cost-effective work-sharing schemes. But all these desirable changes are impossible unless there is a very close identity of interests in industry between management and the shop floor; no government can afford to introduce expensive structural changes in the labour market if they simply add to unit costs and price British goods out of world markets. Britain needs a fundamental change in attitudes; we need the background of understanding and shared interests that is inherent in the social market. To achieve it, the old adversarial pattern of industrial relations has to be changed, as does the sterile conflict of the old class-based party politics.

CHAPTER TWO

The High-Tech Revolution

In strategy there are various timing considerations. From the outset you must know the applicable timing and the inapplicable timing, and from among the large and small things and the fast and slow timings find the relevant timing, first seeing the distance timing and the background timing.

Miyamoto Musashi, *A Book of Five Rings*, 1645

At the end of the Second World War, Britain was still a great industrial power, but since then our decline has gathered momentum. In 1955, our share of the world market for manufactured goods was 19.9 per cent; in 1983 it was 7.4 per cent. Over the same period France, West Germany and Japan rebuilt their devastated industries and then overtook us.

The reasons for our decline are deep-seated. One of the most significant is that Britain produces far too many scientists and not enough engineers, and the consequences have been far-reaching and severe. The House of Lords Select Committee on Science and Technology was told in 1982, when it was collecting evidence for its report *Engineering Research and Development* (March 1983), that the ratio of science to engineering graduates in Britain was 3:1 whereas the ratio in Japan was 0.4:1. This imbalance in Britain is historically due to the fact that the manufacturing industries which required engineers developed their own education and training systems, based on day-release, night schools and craft-derived apprenticeship schemes, during the mid nineteenth century when the universities were neither able nor interested in turning engineering into a profession.

When, after the First World War, the universities started to develop engineering, they started from the base which they knew and had already developed – science; university engineers had to face the opposition of those who had come up the traditional 'hard way'. By contrast the Technische Hochschule in Germany and the Grandes Écoles in France were being established at about the same time, to produce highly trained engineers who would establish – behind protective tariff barriers – the industries that would later compete effectively with the still fundamentally Victorian British industry.

British firms responded by hiring science graduates from the universities and then turning them into engineers. However, this meant that the R & D departments of many British firms were much more inclined to produce new inventions and new products rather than engineering-based improvements of existing products. This trend was compounded during the Second World War, when it was claimed that British scientific work on radar, the Colossus decoding machine, the atomic bomb and sonar made a decisive contribution to winning the war.

However, in the post-war period the real commercial return has gone not to those countries who have been the first to introduce a new product, but to those who have made well-established products available to a mass, often world, market – for example, automobiles, aeroplanes, washing machines, refrigerators, computers and videos. The vast majority of the Japanese R & D effort, for instance, has been not only commercial in orientation but directed at improving on or advancing existing technology. By contrast the USA, France and, above all, Britain were extraordinarily fertile in giving birth to 'radical breakthrough' innovations. Between 1953 and 1973 56 per cent of the British R & D budget was devoted to such innovations and only 4 per cent to improvements of existing technologies. Japanese output in this most 'creative', research-related area was only 8 per cent, whereas 54 per cent of its effort was devoted to developing existing technologies. The problem for Britain is that few commercial profits follow quickly from 'radical breakthroughs'; instead these have tended to produce Concordes, Rolls-Royce RB-211 jet engines, the TSR2, the hovercraft, etc., and large financial losses. The singularly weak British and French performance in the domain of lower-cost and higher-return incremental improvements has created a succession of opportunities for the Japanese and the West Germans, who have concentrated on development rather than innovation.

One important element in Japan's industrial success has been the fact that they have not developed armaments since 1945. By contrast, Britain's relative industrial failure can be attributed in part to the policies of successive governments which have led us to spend about half of our total R & D expenditure on defence-related projects, often of the most innovative variety, such as the Harrier Jump-Jet. Sixty per cent of all British electronic engineers, probably representing 80 per cent of the best engineers, work on defence-related projects. This imbalance would not be so serious if Britain could, like France, sell a good part of its military equipment overseas. Often our equipment is not well enough designed – in itself an engineering failure – for world markets, and our marketing efforts have frequently been poor and have lacked government support. Not surprisingly, perhaps, the 1979 Finniston Report, proposing a major reform of the engineering profession and its industrial influence, has so far not been implemented.

On another front, the government permitted the University Grants Committee in July 1981 to carry on the traditional policy of favouring science over engineering by refusing to implement recommendations to set up an industrial seed-corn fund to support basic research. The Department of Education, with the support of the UGC, fought hard against the recommendations because the fund would have been distributed to the universities in proportion to their earnings from industrial consultancies and contracts, and not by the traditional peer-review mechanism. This change would clearly also have broken the stranglehold that academic scientists have on such engineering research as is done in the universities.

The shortcomings of British engineering, compared with the successes of British science, are nothing new. The Playfair Commission described the superiority of German engineers in 1852. The Devonshire Commission reported in 1885 that the largest single engineering faculty in the world, which used English as a medium of instruction, was at the Imperial University of Tokyo. Perhaps the problems merely seem more glaring today, because the weaknesses of British design and research have contributed to our declining competitiveness in world markets. We are still ignoring the warning of the Finniston Report that, unless urgent action is taken to advance the engineering dimension of our national economic life, industrial decline is inevitable.

Why has our decline as a trading power been so fast? It is not simply the high price of the goods we sell or a lack of ability to market them effectively overseas, although these have not helped. The harsh truth is that we have not invested enough in new industries and technologies and we have failed to invest in the high-quality, up-to-date products which consumers, British or foreign, want to buy. This trend will bring industrial disaster if it is not halted. We must turn round and fight – first to hold, and then gradually to increase, our share of world markets. The alternative is to continue to slither towards the status of an under-developed country without even the excuse of never having been anything else.

The climate has yet to be created for a truly modern economy in Britain. The Labour Party, anti-market, anti-profit, anti-capital as it is, cannot hope to champion the sunrise industries of the future. Those industries are entrepreneurial. They are not bogged down by bureaucracy, cautious, hemmed around with controls, but profit-orientated, fast-moving, dynamic and adventurous. The Labour government after 1945 rightly challenged the power of exploitative mine and steel owners but they put in their place the dead hand of the state. Power in these industries went not to the people who worked in them and managed them, but to Whitehall and Westminster. Individual flair and imagination were stifled by state control and intervention. As a nation we must break out of the fossilized political attitudes that inevitably accompany state control, whether economic or political. For our recovery we must end the centralized power of Whitehall and Westminster and cease to be debilitatingly locked into the dogmas and the politics of the 1940s. As a nation we have to secure a bigger market share of the worldwide growth industry, microelectronic technology.

The alternative is to resist change. It is to defend every job irrespective of subsidy or sense, as was done for steel in the 1970s. Instead of adjusting slowly to necessary change, the industry was drastically pruned in a rush in the early 1980s, with savage social consequences. The Labour Party now fights every pit closure as if it never had closed a pit when in government, is suspicious of every modernization and dissipates its political energy and influence by encouraging the trade unions to defend the past instead of championing the future. Britain has to break out of the old dependence on smoke-stack industries and promote new industries, new jobs and a new environment.

The assertion that encouraging rapid technological development can create jobs rather than destroy them is not readily accepted in the Britain of today, where computers and robots are widely perceived to destroy jobs – indeed their use has convinced people that high unemployment, associated with advancing technology, is now permanently with us. On the contrary, a sustainable reduction in unemployment can only be secured if we adopt advancing technology more quickly than we have in the past, and hence establish a hard core of highly competitive exporting industries capable of competing with imports and generating the wealth to support jobs in other parts of the economy. The historical experience of this and other countries is that employment in manufacturing is declining and employment in the service sector – both the service industries and the public services – is rising. But employment in the service sector will only continue to increase at an adequate rate in Britain if our trading industries are able to hold their own in the world.

Take a particularly stark example, a factory which makes cars. It employs 200,000 people. It produces cars to the value of £1bn per year. But it has been losing the competitive battle for some time. Profits are low – in fact, they have all but disappeared. Funds are not available for investing in the robotics necessary to reduce unit costs to levels which will enable the factory to compete and become profitable again. Unaided, it will gradually die and the jobs will go for ever. The balance of payments will be worse off, since exports will be lost and cars will be imported to help fill the gap in the domestic market. If the experience described is common to a number of industries, the exchange rate will tend to sink and the government will be forced on to the defensive, cutting back its own spending to regulate the balance of payments and stabilize the exchange rate. More jobs will thus be lost in the public services. As their spending power is reduced, other domestic industries will be weakened in turn. It is a vicious spiral, and fairly typical of the British experience over the last ten years.

Suppose on the other hand that this ailing car factory is provided by government with financial assistance, whether by tax incentives or grant aid, to enable it to undertake the investment in robotics which is needed if it is to compete successfully once again. Turnover is maintained at £1bn per year, but the first and most visible effect of the sudden introduction of the robots is that the number of employees is cut from 200,000 to 100,000. A watching public concludes that advancing technology has put 100,000 people out of work. But the restoration of competitiveness has a number of beneficial effects too. First, as unit costs fall, because the workforce has been reduced, output starts expanding again. Turnover rises to £1.25bn over the next few years. Another 25,000 people are then taken on. The balance of payments starts to strengthen, with exports rising and imports going down, by £0.25bn, with the result that – without the inflationary consequences which would flow from a falling exchange rate – government can either lower taxes or expand its own spending. If it increases public spending, especially capital spending, it can do so by four or five times this amount – since this sort of spending has a low import content – without weakening the overall balance of payments position. According to recent figures, increased capital spending of this order generates, for example, 40,000 jobs after two years, 60,000 after three and 75,000 after four. As a result, the introduction of the new technology enables the initial rise in unemployment, which occurred when the robots went in, to be reversed within three to four years, leaving everyone in secure jobs. Had the government stood aside, however, not assisting with the introduction of the new technology, the result would have been snowballing unemployment. More important, the same result will occur if the government does not take the opportunities created by the new technologies to increase its capital spending in other parts of the economy. Unemployment is not a product of there not being enough jobs to be done. To achieve the social objectives we seek in health, education and housing, we need to employ many more people in these areas. But their jobs have to be paid for in the long term by building dynamic competitive industries with high-quality products to sell.

It is necessary to spell out this process because it is so little understood. It explains why Japan for instance, with the most advanced technology in the world, has such low unemployment. Between 1972 and 1982, 8.2 per cent of Japan's manufacturing workforce left the manufacturing sector as compared with 8.4 per cent in Britain, yet today Japan's unemployment rate is 3 per cent whereas ours is nearly 13 per cent. Why? Because in Japan over this period new technologies were rapidly introduced, output per person in the manufacturing sector increased by 32 per cent, and the additional wealth that this produced was used to create 3.6 million new service jobs. Interestingly, in Britain over this period output per person in the manufacturing sector increased by only 9.8 per cent, but we still created 2.9 million new service jobs, mostly in the public sector, even though we had not created the wealth to pay for them. The result is that in Japan we see a country developing into a post-industrial society with low levels of unemployment. But in Britain we see a country suffering, without compensating benefits, from the ravages of de-industrialization.

The example of the car factory is in fact the worst sort of case to quantify the impact of new technology, for it causes a big and sudden change, with a massive initial loss of jobs. It is not the typical case: proportionately much smaller job losses would normally be involved, and where government and industry, working together in a new partnership, develop new activities and products, there would not be this initial loss of jobs to counter the economy-wide gain in jobs which the growth of successful competitive industry makes possible. In general resources can be switched more quickly and easily from declining to expanding activities with much less unemployment all round. But government must take the lead in creating the right climate for technological change by explaining this process and convincing public opinion of its benefits.

As a result of this 'technology-push' strategy, if we were able to raise the average rate of technical advance in industry as a whole by around 2 per cent a year, a small fraction of the sort of advance described in the example, the resulting increase in competitiveness, according to government figures based on the National Economic Development Organization model, would be such as to reduce unemployment by between 550,000 and 850,000 over five years. The jobs created would be real and lasting. It is therefore essential to kill the myth that technology results in fewer jobs, not more, along with the damaging and dogmatic assertion that the best thing government can do is to leave the microchip to its own devices. We can create a dynamic partnership between government and industry, aimed at putting Britain at the forefront of technological advance and investing the proceeds in the jobs of the future.

It is greatly encouraging that Britain is a country whose people are willing to get to grips with the possibilities of the new technologies. We have the highest ownership of home computers in the world – and not just for children to play video games. Recent evidence shows that more and more adults are using home computers as helpful contributors to their daily lives. What is more, it is really quite remarkable that this very rapid penetration into our homes should have taken place in a period of deep recession.

It is, however, not possible to be equally impressed with the performance of British industry in responding to the same opportunities. We hear much about the almost Luddite attitudes of some trade unionists to the introduction of new technologies. Less is said about the equally intractable, and equally damaging attitudes of some of Britain's middle and senior management. Too often, it seems as if much of our industry is trying to shape a new world with old visions.

A report, *Attitudes to New Technology*, published in 1984 by the management and technical consultants, P A Technology, for which 513 company directors from the United States, Australia, Belgium, Britain and West Germany were interviewed, revealed that Britain was at the bottom of the league when it came to applying the latest technology. Polls showed that less than 20 per cent of British firms had made any significant change in their products or production processes in the past five years. By contrast, 44 per cent of Germans, 42 per cent of Americans, 38 per cent of Belgians and 25 per cent of Australians thought new technologies had made a big effect on their production systems. More worrying for the future was that the number of British managers with a defined strategy for innovation was well below the number of German or Belgian managers but, surprisingly, just above the Americans. The much-talked-about high-tech revolution has yet to happen in Britain; we have moved too slowly and too hesitantly to keep up with our competitors.

Too much of British industry is still concentrating on developing products and current technologies for existing markets. This is a strategy for stagnation and decline in the long term. Too many British companies have failed to recognize that true innovation has two cutting edges – one to use new technologies to improve our competitiveness in new markets, the other to push back the frontiers and develop new products to enter totally different markets. Even when we do use new technologies it is too often only to do a little better what we are doing already – to play old tunes on our new fiddles.

What is needed is a basic change in management attitudes towards technical innovation. British firms need to develop positive strategies to push forward at the cutting edge of high technology. That is where the real growth and prosperity of the future lies.

Britain's debate about the inadequacy of government support for civil research and development – in and out of the universities – has been put into sharp focus internationally by the latest report on research by the Organization for Economic Cooperation and Development (OECD) in its 1984 assessment, *Science and Technology Indicators*, which shows that when it comes to civil research Britain is slipping badly.

It is argued by those seeking additional support for R & D, whether through the research councils, university block grants, or joint government sponsorship with industry, that the quality and adequacy of the general fabric of strategic research is the real indicator – and the real breeding ground – of tomorrow's ability to create new wealth. At the heart of this argument is the tacit belief that any nation wise enough to invest enough in its own research effort to use its creative resources to the full, must also be wise enough to steer investment into the areas of the greatest future industrial and commercial promise. But is this the right way to proceed, the critics used to ask, pointing to Japan which buys in its knowhow and is currently beating the rest of the world in every high-tech market that really matters. This viewpoint, which in essence reflects the present government's belief that research should be left entirely to the discretion of industry, is shown in the OECD report to have damaging consequences for the amount and quality of research undertaken in Britain.

There are many ways of looking at a nation's investment in

R & D – as a per capita expenditure, for instance, or as a percentage of either total government expenditure or GDP. By using statistics of this kind the government can and does create a league table of sorts which shows that Britain's *total* R & D expenditure expressed as a percentage of GDP ranks an impressive fourth in the international table, beaten only by the United States, Switzerland, and West Germany. But using the same type of analysis for *civil* research and development reveals a different picture. Britain is seventh in the league on the basis of percentage of GDP and tenth in terms of expenditure per capita. Among the nations now ahead of us, as well as the United States, Germany and Japan, are Switzerland, Sweden, France, Norway and Belgium.

How can this have come about when, in terms of total expenditure, Britain's investment in R & D has increased steadily since the mid-1970s, especially when measured as the public sector percentage of total government expenditure? The answer is that defence takes much of this investment; Britain now lies second to the United States in per capita expenditure on military R & D – about £35 per head a year compared with £48 in the USA. Japan, Germany and France, among others, all spend less on defence and a good deal more on supporting the new high-tech industries in the civil sector. Measured as a proportion of all government expenditure on research the situation is even worse. The OECD report says flatly that by the end of the last decade Britain had become the most defence-orientated country in the OECD area when measured in terms of the percentage of all government R & D funding going into military programmes.

These percentages may explain more about the differences between nations' performances in civil world markets than governments like to pretend. Japan does not separate its defence expenditure, but of total expenditure R & D is now estimated as about 15 per cent. West Germany spends about 17 per cent on defence and France spends nearly 38 per cent. In 1980 – the latest figure quoted in the OECD report – Britain spent 59 per cent of all government expenditure on R & D in the military sector, 5 per cent more than the United States in the same year and 7 per cent more than we were spending on defence in 1975.

A further problem is that too much money is spent in Britain on large research projects without much thought of economic return.

Science policy is a good illustration of this. In 1982 Britain spent £498m on basic scientific research, and the decisions about how that money was distributed were made by the Advisory Board for the Research Councils. This body of scientists and civil servants allocated half the money to the Science and Engineering Research Council (SERC) which funds chemistry, computing, mathematics and engineering. But the lion's share of the SERC budget was spent not in areas most likely to assist British industry but on prestigious 'big science' projects – in nuclear physics and astronomy – which require large and expensive facilities. For example, £48m was spent on astronomy but only £2.4m on robotics; £45m was spent on nuclear physics compared with a bio-technology budget of £1.4m.

The Research Councils are only one leg of the stool on which our public science policy is based. The second leg is the University Grants Committee, which in 1982 distributed nearly £1bn between Britain's forty-five universities and colleges. But it also had the task of overseeing, under government pressure, a 17 per cent reduction in university budgets for 1983–5. It was the way the reduction was allocated by the UGC which damaged university science; those universities where science has the strongest links with industry, like Salford, Aston, Keele and Bradford, taken together had 37 per cent of their gross budget cut. The highest was Salford, with a 44 per cent cut, the lowest was Keele with a 31 per cent cut. By contrast, the combined Oxford and Cambridge budget was reduced by 15.2 per cent. The damage to science was compounded by the way the universities administered the cuts within their own walls. Science is a capital-intensive area, so closing a laboratory for a relatively small number of biotechnology students may enable a course for a hundred history students to continue.

The labyrinthine system of decision-making results in institutional inertia, militates against major change and blocks useful prosperity-oriented experimentation. For instance, one of the reasons for the problems of biotechnology at present is that there are too many people involved in organizing it: the three research councils of medicine, agriculture and science and engineering, the universities and the government Departments of Industry, Energy, the Environment and Agriculture. There is no single body taking a strategic view of our national needs in this area, as do MITI in Japan and the CNRS in France.

Whitehall represents the third leg of the stool on which science policy is based. There is too great a discrepancy between the scientific clout of the Ministry of Defence and that of every other scientific organization in Britain. All government departments allocate part of their budgets to various scientific projects which they believe to be important to their future – and present – tasks. In 1982 the DHSS *Annual Report* disclosed that £22m had been spent on scientific activities. The Department of Energy spent £260m, mostly on atomic energy. By comparison, the Defence Ministry spent £1.85bn, which was three times as much as the total expenditure of the Research Councils.

Another problem is that in the near future there will be shortages of science students and teachers. Although the number of graduates will have risen in total, for all subjects, by an average 31 per cent between 1979 and 1984, in science and technology the increase will have been only 22 per cent. More serious still, in some subjects the total output will have declined. For example, in metallurgy there were 431 graduates in 1970 but there will be only 290 in 1984, while in mechanical engineering the fall will be from 1,738 in 1979 to 1,495 in 1984. From 1985 onwards graduate output will fall by 8 per cent and employers, especially of science and engineering graduates, will face major recruiting problems with growing shortages of skilled labour.

At the heart of the trouble is a shortage of new teaching appointments in science at the universities and colleges. It is estimated that by 1987 there will be 1,250 too few jobs for young science academics, given the effects of government cutbacks and the fact that the cuts fell disproportionately on the science sector of university budgets. Specifically, it is calculated that there will be by 1987 a shortfall of 200 young academics in the biological sciences. In fact the government have acted to try and reverse this trend. In January 1983 a programme for the transfusion of 'new-blood' appointments was announced – nearly £4m extra recurrent grants were made available for the 1983–4 academic year to recruit some 230 additional lecturers, of whom 200 were to be recruited in the natural sciences and technologies. While this is an important corrective step by the government, the evidence suggests that it will still fall short of what is needed to prevent job shortages and skill shortages.

The trends are clear and ominous. Britain is spending substantially less on research relating to industry, health, the environment and new resources, such as renewable energy, than any other nation in the OECD. The 'crowding out' effect is real and the imbalance between the defence and civil portions of total R & D expenditure has grown worse in the last ten years. If a country's future ability to compete and market new products is related, however indirectly, to its current investment in research and development, Britain is on the wrong track.

A sustained improvement in our industrial competitiveness can only be secured if we adopt and exploit advanced technology much more quickly than we have in the past. The countries of Europe must combine to respond to the challenge from Japan and the United States over the application of new technology. A priority here is greater collaboration among European firms, particularly in joint ventures to produce the goods and services of the future. There are certain sectors in which this is starting to happen, such as biotechnology and telecommunications. We need the procurement strength of Europe's wider market and we need Europe's wider research base in science and technology. We cannot compete from a British base alone, but even within Europe Britain must do more. We need to build on new initiatives – such as British Aerospace's development of pressure control valves and autopilot electronics for the European Arianespace Satellite launcher – and learn the lesson of why we failed to see the commercial potential of the space satellite programme and acquiesced in it being so dominated by the French.

Despite the scientific successes secured by individual European countries there is growing evidence that in a number of fields the sum total of European scientific research is not reaching the critical level that will yield a proper economic and industrial return. Europe is by no means lagging behind its competitors in terms of total expenditure on R & D. We are not short of resources or manpower, by comparison. But we are falling behind in key sectors, like computers and agricultural food technology. What is going wrong?

According to the European Commission there has been a decline in the creativeness of our researchers as a result of insufficient multi-disciplinary research just when many fields need to be approached from several angles at the same time. If some of the duplication of work among the different Community countries – all too frequently chasing the same results – could be avoided, more useful research might be done. Equally if more attention was given to the dissemination and use of the fruits of European research, the Community would be in a stronger position. The emergence of a coordinated science policy for the European Community as a whole has been slow. The exploitation of nuclear fusion is one of the few fields in which research being carried out in the Community is closely integrated. European governments have joined forces to build in Britain one of the most powerful experimental installations in the world, the JET (Joint European Torus), which is similar in its technical conception to future fusion reactors. Whatever the outcome of JET scientifically, the project is already assured of a reputation as a triumph of European technological cooperation.

It is sometimes forgotten that Europe was at the forefront of scientific discovery and development long before the post-war creation of the European Economic Community. Each one of the four largest countries of the Community can claim a historically unique role in advancing the frontiers of modern science. In the sixteenth century Italy led the way, from Leonardo da Vinci (1452–1519), who outlined theories of the movement of the earth and the tides and designed a flying machine, to Galileo Galilei (1564–1642), who proved that the earth was neither flat nor at the centre of the universe but revolving about the sun in a Milky Way composed of countless suns and stars.

The mantle of science passed to Britain in the seventeenth century with William Harvey (1578–1657), who demonstrated the circulation of blood, and Sir Isaac Newton (1642–1727), who discovered the laws of gravity. The foundation of the Royal Society of London for Improving Natural Knowledge in 1660 and the Royal Observatory in 1675 marked the time when science became institutionalized. By the late eighteenth century the leadership in scientific thought had passed to France. Antoine Lavoisier (1743–94), the 'father of modern chemistry', outlined the theory of combustion and André-Marie Ampère (1775–1836) pioneered the study of electrodynamics and gave his name to the unit by which an electric current is measured today. The Curies, Pierre (1859–1906) and Marie (1867–1934), discovered radium, and Louis Pasteur (1822–95) developed inoculation and pasteurization. In the nineteenth and early twentieth centuries Germany replaced France as the pre-eminent nation in scientific advance. Two theories from Germany overthrew the very principles on which knowledge of the physical world had been based: the theory of relativity, first elaborated by Albert Einstein in 1905, and the quantum theory, first propounded by Max Planck in 1900.

In the last eighty years, despite the competition from new and vigorous scientific communities with large resources in the United States and the Soviet Union, the scientific tradition has continued to make itself felt in modern Europe with Britain again playing a leading role. One important index is the number of Nobel Prizes for science won by the leading scientific countries of the world. Between 1901 and 1981, Britain (47), Germany (46) and France (20) have won a total of 113 prizes in physics, chemistry and physiology or medicine, compared with 98 prizes won by the United States (85) and the Soviet Union (13). Furthermore, Europe has maintained its proportion of Nobel Laureates in the second half of the century at nearly the same level as in the first half.

British scientists have some reason to be proud of their international achievements. Since 1901 they have won a sixth of the scientific Nobel Prizes. Some of the highlights from the long list are: splitting the atom (Rutherford), the development of penicillin (Fleming), the discovery of radar (Blackett), jet propulsion (Whittle), the hovercraft (Cottrell). The ability of Europe to compete effectively in pure research with the great institutions of the United States and the Soviet Union has owed a large intellectual debt to the originality and dedication of Britain's academic scientists.

Unfortunately, in science as in so many other fields, Britain's lukewarm attitude to European cooperation has meant making heavy weather, apart from JET, of other collaborative ventures. For instance, Britain's continued membership of the European Molecular Biology Laboratory, based at Heidelberg, the main offshoot of the European Molecular Biology Organization, has been constantly in doubt. On three separate occasions in the last ten years the British Medical Research Council has reviewed its continuing membership of the Laboratory. This has served merely to undermine a collaborative institution that could enliven European molecular biology.

New opportunities will arise in the future for greater European cooperation and partnership in scientific research. Britain must become more wholehearted and enthusiastic. This year, for the first time, the Community will incorporate all its research, development and demonstration (R D & D) activities in a new programme, laying down its strategy for 1984–7. This is an important milestone, both because the European Community is greatly increasing the money for these activities and because this higher expenditure is accompanied by an unprecedented effort to define the main goals of Community-financed science and technology programmes and the balance to be maintained between the various sectors. Resources will no longer be handed out piecemeal according to the circumstances of the moment.

For the four years covered by the FAST programme (Forecasting Assessment in Science and Technology), the plan is to allocate 3,750m ECU at constant 1983 prices. This is 940m ECU p.a., compared with the 600m ECU actually spent last year, representing a growth of about 50 per cent without allowing for inflation. In relative figures, the research sector received 2.6 per cent of the Community budget in 1983 while the figure for 1987 is to be 4 per cent.

The programme defines four broad areas requiring further scientific research. The first concerns agriculture and the production of biomass as a fuel crop on marginal soils; the second concerns industry and the promotion of integrated flexible manufacture and software; the third concerns the management of raw materials and the efficiency of extraction processes; the fourth concerns the improvement of energy resources. The programme says that before JET reaches the industrial stage, 100,000m ECU will have to be spent worldwide. The size of that expenditure underscores the direction of European cooperation.

The programme, outlining in embryo a Community science policy with sufficient resources to make it work, is only a beginning, although it stands a chance of being much more than that. The Commission hopes that the national governments will do more than use the programme as a basis for their own policies. It could also stimulate discussion within each ministry on programmes and priorities for the individual member state. Above all, the FAST programme should be constantly borne in mind in international negotiations, in order to harmonize the various policies and avoid the frequent duplication of work that handicaps European research in comparison with the Americans and the Japanese.

The FAST programme offers Europe a coherent guide for the future direction of scientific research and discovery. It highlights the fact that Europe will have to find ways of adapting continuously to technological change. With a long tradition of leading the world in pure scientific discovery, Europe should take this opportunity to establish a new set of collaborative ventures in those areas of scientific R & D vital for our future. Science is the gateway for technological advance – there is no guarantee that its discoveries will be put to use – but without that basis of new thought and knowledge we cannot hope to win back the position of industrial and economic leadership that was once Europe's hallmark. In Britain it is worth reminding ourselves that some projects have to be organized on a scale far beyond the boundaries of a single state. Such is the case for science. It needs the breadth and strength of the European Community if it is to continue to match the range and endeavour of the scientific and technological effort of the two superpowers, the US and the USSR.

CHAPTER THREE

Public Expenditure Priorities

It is a complete mistake to believe that there is a dilemma between schemes for increasing employment and schemes for balancing the Budget . . . Quite the contrary. There is no possibility of balancing the Budget except by increasing the national income, which is much the same as increasing employment.

John Maynard Keynes, *The Means to Prosperity*, 1933

Over the last couple of decades there has been a considerable growth in the role of the state in the economy of all the industrial- ized western countries. It is not just Britain that faces this problem and it is worth first examining this trend in its international context. The growth of the state's role is reflected in the increasing ratio of total government expenditure to national income (GDP). The seven main industrialized western countries taken together showed a rise in government expenditure from 28.7 per cent in 1960 to 32.6 per cent in 1970 and 40.6 per cent in 1982 – a rise of 41 per cent over the whole twenty-two-year period. For the United States and Japan, the shares in 1982 were virtually identical, at about 35.5 per cent; but for the US this represented a rise of 28 per cent from the 1960 figure of 27.8 per cent, whereas for Japan it represented a rise of 92 per cent, from a 1960 figure of only 18.3 per cent. In the four big European countries, the 1982 share ranged from 46.5 per cent in Britain to 54 per cent in Italy. For Italy, this represented a 79 per cent increase since 1960; for Britain, France and Germany the rise was in the range of 47–51 per cent. In Canada the 1982 figure was 46.4 per cent – a 61 per cent rise since 1960. The broad outline of what is an international trend is that in the US and Japan the government is spending a little over a third of the national income, while in Europe and Canada the figure is closer to half. The increase in this ratio has been slow in the United States, fast in Japan, and somewhere in between in Europe and Canada.

A number of factors underlie this rising share of the national income spent by the government. One is the fact that as societies grow wealthier, they demand more services, such as better roads or cleaner air, which can often only be provided by state action. A more significant factor, because it is inescapable, has been the ageing of the population. As the proportion of the population over sixty-five and over eighty rises, expenditure on state retirement pensions rises too, as does government expenditure – where government finances them – on the personal social services, residential homes and geriatric wards required by the elderly. A third factor in the rise in public expenditure as a share of the national income is the so-called 'relative price effect': because the scope for raising productivity in many parts of the public sector is quite limited, the price of public sector output rises, at any given inflation rate, relative to the price of private sector output, and this will result in a rising ratio of public expenditure at current prices even if in real terms the share of the public sector remains the same. A fourth factor is of more recent origin and, it is to be hoped, of less permanent duration. Rising unemployment has increased government expenditure on social security benefits, particularly in Europe, while in some recent years real GDP has been stagnant or falling. The effect of each factor has been to raise the share of the national income devoted to public expenditure.

Whatever the precise mixture of reasons for the rapid growth in public expenditure over the past couple of decades, one consequence has been a rise in the burden of taxation. In Europe total tax revenue as a percentage of GDP rose from 27.8 per cent in 1965 to 34.4 per cent in 1975 and 37.5 per cent in 1981. In Canada it rose at much the same rate from 25.9 per cent of GDP in 1965 to 32.9 per cent in 1975 and 34.7 per cent in 1981. In the US the rise was considerably slower – from 26.5 per cent in 1965 to 30.2 per cent in 1975 and 31.2 per cent in 1981. In Japan, on the other hand, it was considerably faster: it rose from only 17.8 per cent in 1965 to 21 per cent in 1975 and 26.9 per cent in 1981.

The widespread view that high taxes were inhibiting investment and growth has led in the last few years to vigorous efforts by most industrialized governments to cut back public expenditure. But the underlying factors making for rising public expenditure are powerful and pervasive; they consist not only of the all-important demographic trends but also of such factors as rapidly rising American defence expenditure and a high level of agricultural and industrial subsidies in Europe. To slow down or even halt the rising share of national income taken by public expenditure will be very difficult.

Two demographic trends of paramount importance need to be examined in more detail. First, the post-war baby boom was followed virtually everywhere by a marked decline in the birthrate. In North America, this decline dates from the late 1950s, in Europe from the early 1960s. In Japan there was a very steep decline in the birthrate during the first half of the 1950s, followed by a further decline since the early 1970s. One effect of this has been – and will continue to be – a marked slowing-down in the growth of total population. Another has been a rise in the proportion of the population which is of working age, as those born during the baby boom have moved into the labour force. This factor should have had a favourable effect on growth rates and living standards, particularly since those in the 15–24 age group are more willing and able than older workers to move into sectors and areas where the demand for labour is rising. Unfortunately, the relatively slow growth in the demand for labour since the mid-1970s has largely dissipated this asset.

The second key demographic trend is that the population of the western industrialized countries is an ageing population. Between 1960 and 1980 the proportion of the European population aged sixty-five and over rose from 10.5 per cent to 13.5 per cent, though for the time being the rise has levelled off. The proportion in North America rose from about 9 per cent to about 10.5 per cent over the same period, and is continuing to rise. In Japan the proportion of the population aged 65 and over was in 1960 only about 6 per cent – but rose rapidly to almost 9 per cent in 1980. This rapid rise will continue; by the end of the century the proportion of the Japanese population in this age group is expected to have reached about 15 per cent, considerably higher than in North America. A particular problem is posed by the very old – those aged eighty and over – since the proper care of this age group is very expensive in terms of medical treatment and residential accommodation. The number of people in this category in the OECD countries as a whole grew from 12 million in 1970 to nearly 16 million in 1980; and is expected to be little short of 21 million by 1990.

However justified the reasons for these increases in public expenditure may be, the fact remains that expenditure on this scale can only be financed by a combination of taxation and government borrowing that can have adverse effects on the operation of market economies. High taxes can inhibit saving and investment, and discourage the innovation, risk-taking and entrepreneurial drive which underlie economic progress and increasing prosperity. High levels of government borrowing can lead to either high interest rates, which may crowd out productive private sector investment, or to increases in the money supply, which may fuel inflation. In Britain there has been a tendency to believe that North Sea oil revenues shield us from the necessity to examine public expenditure growth critically – but this is a dangerous assumption, as is explained later.

The dangers of continuing public expenditure growth have been increasingly recognized in recent years by western industrial governments, whether of the right or the left, and though attempts have been made to cut back public expenditure as a share of the national income, so far little success has been achieved. Part of the reason for this lies in a 'can't win' situation: cuts in public expenditure which, in the short run at any rate, result in people becoming unemployed instead of moving into the private sector of the economy, depress the national income while at the same time adding to state payments of social security benefits. But there are deeper reasons than this. The hard choices that must be made are often electorally unpopular and are, therefore, not being made. Agricultural and industrial subsidies which should have been phased down and in some cases removed entirely are still being paid. Declining industries which should have been allowed to die are being kept alive. Social security benefits which should have been concentrated on those in need are going indiscriminately to the better-off as well. Though the nature of the choices may differ somewhat between countries, all countries are tending to suffer because of the interrelated nature of our economies.

In the United States, taxes have been cut, particularly for the higher-income groups; social security payments have risen rapidly, as have interest payments on the national debt; and very large increases in defence expenditure have been undertaken. The consequence in 1984 was a budget deficit of some $200bn, equivalent to over 5 per cent of the GNP. Paradoxically, this has provided the US with a Keynesian-type fiscal stimulus which has led to a rapid revival of the economy; but the combination of a low American propensity to save and a tight control of the growth of the money supply has meant very high real interest rates not only in the US itself, where the costs to borrowers have until very recently been muted by a comprehensive system of tax relief on interest payments, but around the world. In the interests of both the American economy and the global economy something has to give; either the rapid growth of US defence expenditure must be cut back – by sharing the burden more equally across the NATO countries or by negotiating conventional and nuclear arms reductions which would not endanger the security of the West – or US non-defence expenditure must be cut back; or taxation levels must be increased. Indeed this is probably an understatement; the scale of the problem is such that action on all three fronts is needed as a matter of urgency.

In Europe, the situation is not very different. The rapidly rising prosperity which occurred during the twenty-five years after the immediate post-war recovery permitted the creation of an ambitious nexus of social services. To a high degree, European countries provide free or subsidized health and educational services and generous benefits for retired people, the unemployed and sick, and disadvantaged groups of other kinds. The financing of these expenditures out of taxation and employers' and employees' social security contributions, feasible in a buoyant and rapidly growing economy, has been progressively harder to accomplish as growth has slowed and the recession has contributed to an inward-looking and less generous mood. This financial burden may well have had significant adverse effects on incentives, competitiveness, investment and growth, and thus be in part responsible for the relative decline of the European economy and of the even more serious relative decline of the British economy within the European Community.

The government has responded in part, as detailed in the National Income and Expenditure Blue Book for 1983/4, by planning to hold overall expenditure steady while continuing to cut capital expenditure. There has been already a long-term and significant fall in general government capital spending from £11bn in 1973 to less than £7bn in 1978 and less than £3bn (at current prices) in 1984. In the last ten years the public sector share of total investment has fallen from 44 per cent to 26 per cent. The reason for this fall, however, has nothing to do with the usefulness or otherwise of public investment. Successive governments have wanted to cut public spending as 'painlessly' as possible. Capital spending has been easier to cut than revenue spending. It loses fewer votes, it cushions us all for the present and allows us to forget the future. The 1976 and 1980 Budgets, under Labour and Conservative governments, are classic examples of this. The 1984 Public Expenditure White Paper shows that despite their large majority the government intends to continue this approach up until the next election. In 1984/5 planned total public sector capital spending will be £400m less, in cash terms, than in 1983/4. Even bigger reductions are planned for 1985/6, and in 1986/7 planned capital spending will be £1.4bn less, in cash terms, than in 1983/4. This is very disturbing. Irrespective of one's party political affiliation it cannot be right to bequeath to the next generation such a legacy of neglect.

We, who are the beneficiaries of vast investment, both public and private, by past generations, are failing to provide the next generation with a basic modern and efficient infrastructure to sustain the economy and industry in the future.

Britain's publicly provided capital infrastructure is deteriorating fast. Immense problems are piling up for generations to come because of neglect today. Hospital and school maintenance budgets, the least glamorous of all expenditure items, are progressively less able to stem the tide of decay. Our man-made waterways are generally about 200 years old, our railways a hundred. Our roads range from two-year-old motorways to ancient tracks that were there before the Roman invasion. The problems of roads are traffic growth, of railways adaptation, of canals straightforward neglect. Transport environmental problems, which are rightly given great attention, are critically linked to the lack of capital. Not all the environmental problems would be solved by greater capital investment, but most would and others would be considerably alleviated.

The huge growth of traffic and the rise in vehicle weights has not been matched by increased capacity and durability of roads, despite annual expenditure of nearly £2bn. The problem is worse around towns and cities where traffic is heaviest. The 1984 Road Maintenance Survey identified the need to improve maintenance and repair for crumbling roads. Improvements have been made for trunk roads, whose maintenance budget in the last ten years rose 30 per cent in cash terms, from £118m to £155m in 1983/4, but not for local roads, whose budget fell over the same period by 12 per cent, from £770m to £680m. Some of our motorways have outlived their designed life and are not suitable for today's loads and speeds. Motorway connections between industrial centres and east-coast ports – some of which are flourishing, though small – are inadequate. The number of route-miles of motorway completed has been falling steadily in recent years from forty-seven in 1979–80 to sixteen in 1982–3.

On the railways, tracks and vehicles have suffered from lack of investment under successive governments as the system's market share fell from 18 to 7 per cent of passengers and 53 to 15 per cent of freight between 1950 and 1980. Under-investment is now compounding the decline. Three thousand miles of track out of a total of 11,000 miles will be unusable by 1990 unless maintenance expenditure is raised, and the entire fleet of 3,000 diesel multiple-unit trains, operating the rural services, will need to be replaced by 1990, at a total cost of around £1bn. This would be in addition to any new investment in rail electrification. The government intend reducing their Public Service Obligation Grant to British Rail from a 'cost ceiling' of £865m in 1984/5 to a planned target of £635m (at current prices) in 1986/7. Even given the improved performance of British Rail recently, this reduction in government grant will leave little room for the additional investment that is needed to improve the quality of the service, despite their cutting back on routes.

Britain's 2,000 miles of man-made waterways have suffered

even greater neglect. There is a future for inland-waterway transport and this was recognized in the Freight Facilities Scheme, started in 1977, to encourage a transfer of freight from road to rail or waterway. Government grants of £33m have been awarded in England (£6m in 1983) with a transfer of about 19m tonnes a year of freight from the roads (nearly 2m tonnes last year). Some expansion of the scheme is planned for the next few years, according to the Public Expenditure White Paper, but to be effective greater attention must be given to the shabby condition of the rail and waterway networks themselves. The British Waterways Board Annual Report in 1983 criticized the government for failing to implement a proper maintenance and repair programme involving, for instance, £5m for bridge repairs; £9m to strengthen bridges so that they can take the bigger lorries authorized by the EEC and the Armitage Report; £4m for repairs to just four of the Board's forty-six active tunnels.

Our sewers – whose state affects our transport system, since they carry waste water under the roads – are mostly brick-lined tunnels up to 200 years old and are in an advanced state of disrepair. They are part of a total supply-and-return water system composed of 750 reservoirs, 2,000 water-treatment works, 170,000 miles of water mains, 130,000 miles of sewers and 6,500 sewage treatment works. The entire system would cost more than £50bn to replace, and much of it is in urgent need of renewal. Manchester, whose exceptionally rapid expansion in the early nineteenth century gave it one of the largest and oldest urban sewerage systems, is an example of the low priority given to sewerage investment. In Manchester a £500m road system receives nearly £5m maintenance a year, while a £900m sewer system receives less than £500,000 a year. That is 0.05 per cent of replacement cost for sewers, against 0.91 per cent for roads.

It has been estimated by the Institute of Fiscal Studies that the public sector's net liabilities may now be growing by as much as £20bn per year, because of inadequate net capital investment, rapidly growing pension liabilities and the forthcoming exhaustion of North Sea oil revenues. Such a view merely reinforces the fact that we are failing to take advantage of the once-in-a-lifetime windfall from North Sea oil. The problem is that we are mixing up our objectives. We are putting £9bn a year derived from North

Sea oil towards the £15bn annual costs of the present level of unemployment. These once-and-for-all oil revenues should be invested in the infrastructure of our future. In some cases – in the construction industry, for example – such investment would reduce unemployment, but other measures, often more effective, are also needed to deal with unemployment. The cost of unemployment should be a charge on our present standards of living, not on the infrastructure essential for future generations. Spending more on our transport infrastructure is totally justified on its own merits and is one of the most productive and essential investments we can make with our North Sea oil revenues. We have a moral responsibility not to go on frittering them away. We are currently mortgaging the future on a scale and in a manner that our children's children will rightly recall with contempt.

It is now clear that we cannot rely for much longer on North Sea oil for at 1984 prices there will be a fall in oil export revenues of over £1bn each year between 1988/9 and 1993/4. By then, the steadily weakening balance of payments position is likely to be associated with a falling real exchange rate, higher inflation and weakening growth.

To understand why, it is first necessary to distinguish between estimates of reserves in the ground and the annual level of production over the next ten years to 1994. The Department of Energy's 1984 revised estimates of reserves puts them in the range of 1,410 to 5,280m tonnes, compared with a range of 1,220 to 4,220m tonnes in last year's report. These figures were hailed as giving a great boost to Britain's future prospects but they carry the caveat that it is more probable that the eventual outcome will be in the lower half of the new range than in the upper half.

Comparison of the two ranges indicates that the lower end has been increased only by a little, the upper end by a great deal. It is not unreasonable to ask why the upper end has been increased in this way. The estimates are divided into two parts. First, there are estimates of 'discovered recoverable reserves' – proven, probable and possible reserves in fields already discovered. In this category, there has been a very small increase in central reserve estimates (some 25m tonnes) since last year. Second, there are 'undiscovered recoverable reserves', the figures for which are highly speculative and relate to undrilled geological structures in the northern North

Sea. In this category, the range of reserves not yet found – which are inherently less soundly based and where the most likely outcomes can be expected to be considerably below the mid-point of the ranges – has been substantially increased, from 200–750m tonnes in the 1983 estimates to 450–1,900m tonnes in 1984, and it is this which accounts for the overall increase. So the hard figures have not changed. Recent optimistic forecasts are founded on nothing more than the fact that there may be more oil to be discovered at some time in the future in the very difficult outward reaches of the North Sea.

Plainly, this does not provide grounds for supposing that the annual level of production from the North Sea is likely to be significantly higher over the next ten years than we previously thought. In relation to production levels, the main points are that any extra oil which there may be in the northern North Sea has not yet been discovered and that discoveries will probably occur piecemeal, which means that most are a number of years away. Even if discovery was followed by an immediate decision to develop, it would be five to seven years before the oil started to flow in significant quantities; development might not in fact take place quickly since discoveries in very difficult areas might not be commercially exploitable. Costs of production are likely to be substantially higher than for existing fields. Already reports suggest that oil from the Magnus field costs $18 a barrel to produce. It could well require a further strengthening of the international oil price before further North Sea oil development becomes worthwhile.

Given the time lags before new discoveries are made, between discoveries and decisions to develop, and between such decisions and the oil actually flowing, it is very unlikely that the upward revision of the fantasy end of the reserves range will significantly affect the projected annual levels of oil production during this Parliament or the next.

Using the government's own procedure and taking the centre of their own published ranges in 1984 we find the following profile for North Sea oil production (in million tonnes):

1982–3	1983–4	1988–9	1993–4
107	118	97.5	65

In broader economic terms, this projected rate of decline of oil production, and hence exports, is deeply disturbing. Expressed in another way it means that net oil exports at their peak will amount in value to about one quarter of our manufactured exports. To fill the hole in the balance of payments as net oil exports fall to zero over the next ten years, industry will have to gear itself up to export 25 per cent more. It is clear that British overseas investment, which it was thought at one time might generate sufficient income to replace lost oil revenues, is turning out to have been insufficient to fulfil this function on its own, so that more exports of traded goods will somehow have to be induced. The main mechanism by which industrial exports will be encouraged will no doubt be a falling exchange rate, and we know from experience that a falling exchange rate is accompanied by manifold dangers for the economy.

The foreign exchange markets will anticipate a prolonged period of sterling weakness and when the change in sentiment occurs the adjustment in the exchange rate will not be slow and smooth. It will be sudden and violent, with the same tendency to overshoot downwards which in 1979 to 1982 it displayed in an upward direction. This will no doubt generate inflation and a subsequent deflationary response from the government. If growth in the 1980s has been sustained at 2–3 per cent, unemployment will still be in the 2.5–3 million range at the end of the decade and this will be the plateau from which it will start to rise remorselessly once again during the coming years of difficulty. The levels it could reach in the 1990s if recession went on for four or five years while the economy adjusted to a loss of exports on this scale are very alarming.

Given this sombre prospect, it is whistling in the dark to boast that Britain has a lot more oil. The harsh reality is that the rate of production of British oil is still slowing down year by year, and it is this which will cause severe economic difficulties in future.

It is disingenuous of the government to suggest that upward revisions in speculative estimates of yet-to-be discovered reserves, which cannot be developed during this Parliament or the next, undermine the view that North Sea oil output will be running down fairly steadily over the next ten years. The government's production assumptions contradict their own publicity.

This makes it all the more necessary for everyone in Britain to reassess objectively not just the capital but the revenue side of public expenditure and the future roles of the private sector. A reassessment will not be easy to achieve, for while the vested interests associated with public sector employment have become very strong, public sector employees do provide essential services for the vast majority of the country. Blaming the people employed in the public sector for all the ills of the British economy is as foolish as believing that public sector employees can escape sustained scrutiny of all their activities. Also, the public sector per se is becoming the victim of an ideological political debate about privatization or nationalization in which the criteria of improving standards of service and cost effectiveness have become secondary to dogmatic assertions of the supposed superiority in all instances of private or state ownership.

The public sector faces now and over the next few years a crisis of confidence. It is being cut back both in the numbers employed and in the rewards paid out to its employees. It may be possible to do one or the other without provoking a deep-seated malaise, but it is not possible to do both. Working in the public sector still carries for many a sense of duty, a sense of responsibility. Society should not lightly dismiss the virtues of a sense of public service, commitment, dedication and, above all, impartiality – virtues which we undermine at our peril. Fair and agreed procedures for fixing pay and conditions for the public service are not minor matters. They guarantee not only smooth working, without disruption, but are part of the underpinning of the independence and integrity of the system.

For the fifth year in a row, the government has arbitrarily set down strict cash limits for the public services. The effects have often been unfair, and the consequences divisive and resented. Calculations by the Institute of Fiscal Studies suggest the 1984/5 public expenditure plans left room for only a 1.9 per cent increase in average pay for the employees of central and local government. In effect, by rate-capping local authorities, the government have put local government employees in virtually the same position as central government public sector employees. Since 1979/80, pay increases in local and central government, including health and education, have been held below those in the rest of the economy. Tight cash limits for the nationalized industries have also increased governmental influence just when the government claims that it is standing aside from the bargaining process. The true position is very different, as was revealed by the recent disclosure of documents showing that the government intervened in the 1984 pay negotiations between British Rail and the railway unions because of their wish to avoid a simultaneous clash with the miners in the coal-industry dispute.

Although the government refuses to admit it openly, they are operating, and have been operating for some time, a public sector incomes policy in all but name. With unemployment so high for the past few years, pay claims have been modest and the government can claim that inflation has come down. But in practice, in 1984, the targets are being increasingly breached, and if they are breached extensively and the process continues, as is likely, into 1985, the outcome will be dangerously inflationary and could lead to further cuts in services and falling standards.

The present practice of setting target figures for the annual round of wage-bargaining is beginning to break down, for targets almost inevitably tend to set a floor to the pay round, and it follows that there is bound to be some upward drift. The 1984 3 per cent target is probably compatible with a 4–5 per cent outcome. The 6 per cent limit for the 1982–3 pay round resulted in an actual increase of 7–8 per cent in money earnings. Each 1 per cent on the public sector wage bill adds £200m to public expenditure, and this is the primary reason behind the government's attempt to hold pay increases down at a low level. It is not just the revenue side of public expenditure that is being squeezed; the capital squeeze is even more intense.

This government has in the past shown itself to be strongly opposed to determining public sector pay by comparing it to wages paid in the private sector. Not only did they abolish the Clegg Commission, but they followed this by scrapping the comparability-based pay system for white-collar civil servants. Comparability machinery has been regarded by this government as an engine of inflation. By contrast, the 1970s, a period dominated by formal and informal pay policies, was a time of real improvement for public sector workers. According to studies carried out by the National Institute of Economic and Social Research on pay comparability and comparisons between grades, almost all major

groups of public sector workers have clearly gained ground against
the private sector since 1972. Public corporation manual workers
earned 15 per cent more than their private sector counterparts, an
improvement of nearly 10 per cent compared to the early seventies.
Non-manual/white-collar workers in the central civil service
earned between 5 and 6 per cent more than their private sector
counterparts, though here the improvement was much lower –
only 2 per cent – as compared with the early seventies.

There are, of course, distortions in such comparisons, not least
because the earnings of private sector manual workers rise less
during recessions and more during periods of growth, thanks to
overtime. Also, non-manual public sector grades have a better
record on equal pay for women, which has boosted its average. But
if the size of the trend can be disputed, the trend itself is un-
mistakable. Similarly, most but not all of the ground gained against
the private sector has been won by public corporation manual
workers (where most of the union growth in the seventies took
place, for example in NUPE and NALGO). In recent years the pay
awards of white-collar public service workers have not kept pace
with the private sector and the result has been a loss of morale as
their lead has been eroded.

Nevertheless, comparability returned in 1982–3 with the
Megaw inquiry into civil service pay, two separate working parties
on comparability for teachers in England and Wales and a new pay
review body for the nurses. These different review bodies are an
invitation to leapfrogging in the pay comparability system. The
armed forces, hitherto exempt from interference by this government, and the doctors and dentists have had their recommendations altered by the government, while the nurses' pay award was
honoured in full. The police have applied for a separate review
board following their substantial increases as a result of an ad hoc
inquiry. The trend is clearly towards comparability but in a very
unsystematic fashion. The Prime Minister's attitude to arbitration
is similarly inconsistent – insisting on an independent arbitrator in
the water dispute in 1983 but refusing any arbitration on the
1984 teachers' dispute until forced to accept it by a majority on
the Burnham Committee. The civil servants have lost their Pay
Research and Arbitration agreement.

The Office of Manpower Economics reported in April 1984 on

current pay movements for white-collar groups in the private sector and the government was embarrassed by the main conclusion of the report that basic pay rates between May 1983 and February 1984 had increased for private sector white-collar workers by 6 per cent, twice the public service pay target of 3 per cent. The report's findings demonstrate the difficulty of using a low pay limit for the public sector as an exhortatory example for the private sector to follow, and hence as part of a general strategy to reduce pay settlement levels in the economy. Public sector pay increases have recently been running at a lower level than private sector ones. The build-up of public sector pay pressure in 1984 is a result of two major problems in the government's approach to the issue. First, there is a clear gap between what the government wants – that public sector pay should be made more responsive to market forces in the private sector – and what it actually gets. Second, it now faces gradual but relentless pressure for a coherent system of pay comparability after three years of low settlements in the public sector.

The government should have implemented the Megaw proposals in 1983; these proposals recommended a new, more market-based system of restricted pay comparability. Instead, the government lost valuable support by attempting to toughen the recommendations of the Megaw inquiry in such a way as to jeopardize the independence and balance of the comparability system proposed by Megaw. Megaw proposed that civil service pay should be determined by the so-called 'inter-quartile' range of outside earnings – the band of pay between 25 and 75 per cent of the whole range of relevant private sector wages. A Pay Information Board would run the system, providing information to both sides on a wide range of issues. These would include the inter-quartile wage comparisons – with major adjustments every four years and minor ones annually.

The challenge is to devise a non-inflationary system of arbitrating over comparability, where the arbitrator is genuinely independent of both the employer, the government and the unions. The obvious way forward for the government would have been to adopt a Megaw-style comparability system but one which started from a lower base so that the likelihood of a clash with cash limits was reduced. Factors like pension contributions and productivity would have also provided the government with some flexibility in negotiation.

Instead, the government agreed that recourse to arbitration must be sanctioned by both sides but they also insisted that any arbitration award could be overridden by Parliament on a motion initiated by the government, while Megaw specifically did not. Megaw had proposed a parliamentary veto, but only on a motion initiated by the Opposition, or by a group of backbenchers. Megaw argued that the government ought not to initiate such a motion as they were a party to the arbitration procedure and outcome. The unions insisted, not unreasonably, that such a veto would render even compulsory arbitration awards meaningless, because in effect the government could scrap any award it did not like, whereas the unions had no choice but to accept. Megaw warned that, without an arbitration procedure which was seen to be balanced and independent by both sides, the chances of securing a stable system of compulsory arbitration and a no-strike agreement with the unions would be significantly reduced.

The unions are not uniformly hostile to the market-related principles advanced by the Megaw Committee. The Institute of Professional Civil Servants and the First Division Association are keen to see them acted upon. The Civil and Public Service Association was less keen, but nonetheless talked to the Treasury and demanded a unilateral right to arbitration, access to the Board's data and many other things. The shifting of civil service unions to the left politically will make it much harder to achieve no-strike agreements and in the aftermath of the GCHQ affair, where the government, without consultation, banned their own employees from continuing as members of trade unions, there is a danger that no-strike agreements will become identified with not having proper trade union representation. Nevertheless, the government could still secure union agreement for a Megaw-style comparability system, providing such a system was balanced and independent, as Megaw recommended, and could not be constantly overruled by the government.

The protracted negotiations on the Megaw Report in 1983 now appear to have stalled. When Ministers were talking about it to their civil service officials, they asked if a longer-term comparability system would mean an annual series of awkward comparisons; 'Yes, Minister,' came the reply – leading to a sudden marked waning of enthusiasm for Megaw as the solution to the problem of settling civil servants' pay.

Private sector pay increases in the next two pay rounds, according to the Income Data Services report last May, will probably remain steady at 5–7 per cent, with a median rise of 5 per cent. If pay comparisons are made primarily with private sector companies, as Megaw suggests, this will mean reasonable but not excessive public sector rises too. Hence, a comparability system – which many public sector unions want – could be used by the government as a means of restraining inflation, rather than as a mechanism for creating it, like the Clegg Commission. Such a system puts the onus on private sector employees to bargain only within market disciplines and it must mean developing a tougher competition policy to prevent monopoly private sector employers simply passing on unjustifiable wage increases in prices. If the mainly private market sector really reflected their true market position in their wage-bargaining, then comparability for the public sector need not be feared. If the private sector allows inflationary wage-bargaining, however, then government should intervene with the mechanism of an inflation tax held in reserve against the possibility of a return, as in 1971/2, to private-sector-led inflation.

A non-inflationary comparability system for the public sector is credible along the lines of the Megaw blueprint. The arbitration procedures suggested by Megaw have great merits provided the government does not constantly interfere with the independence of those procedures. One cannot expect the unions to accept no-strike agreements as an essential part of such procedures, unless the arbitration is to be balanced and free of political interference, as outlined by Megaw. Beyond this, there is a great advantage in establishing a long-term, stable and comprehensive system of pay comparability in the public sector, doing away with the need for the collection of review boards and one-off inquiries characterizing the present ad hoc system of comparability. The aim would be to do this without replacing the bargaining process between employer and employees.

Any government must have a clear view on the pay of its employees. If public sector workers claim excessive increases they will pre-empt government investment or reduce the number of jobs. It is against everybody's interest to force the government into paying for higher inflation. Equally, it is a recipe for disruption to have public sector pay settlements falling continuously behind those at comparable levels in the private sector.

The government can, as any employer would, propose a variety of differential pay movements to reflect the need for, say, more engineers or fewer doctors, and this is compatible with a policy of comparability of incomes. If the government relies too heavily on cash limits to hold the line on public sector pay, and attempts to stand back too far from negotiating with their own workers – a characteristic of the present government in several past disputes – they will ultimately fail to protect the consumer from the monopoly power of public sector workers. Hence it is up to government not only to fix a target – or a norm or a range – for pay rises in the public sector, on an annual basis, but also to determine what institutions are needed to meet such goals.

An independent Public Service Pay Information Board (PSPIB) should be established to define, wherever this is possible, broadly comparable private sector groups in relation to each public service group with which the government will be in negotiation, and to provide data on the movement in pay for the comparative groups in the previous year. Such data will not point to a precise outcome for the pay settlement of each public sector group, since in each case there will be a number of private sector comparators with a range of settlements. But the data would set the framework within which negotiations would take place between the government and each bargaining group.

Pay settlements negotiated on this basis would need to exhibit three vital features. First, they would be determined in accordance with the principle of comparability, so that the system should be accepted as fair by the groups involved. Second, provided that the comparable groups were sufficiently closely defined, settlements would also reflect the balance of demand and supply in the appropriate part of the labour market. Third, taking one year with another, public and private sector pay settlements would be kept broadly in line, to avoid the periodic large catching-up rises which we have known in the past and which invariably give an upward twist to inflation.

Since there would be room for negotiation between the government and public service groups on the basis of the range of comparators supplied by the PSPIB, there would also be room for disagreements. Hence there would be a need to devise arrangements for arbitration which governments would not constantly override, preferably by the introduction of 'pendular', or 'final-offer', arbitration – which does not allow an arbitrator to split the difference and so avoids the open invitation to employees to overbid and employers to underbid.

Within a fair system of comparability, it should be possible to negotiate a number of no-strike agreements. It is in fact only recently that a number of public service groups have acquired the right to strike. Any group will want reasonable terms in exchange for giving up that right. But they might well feel, particularly after recent events, that a comparability formula, plus some agreed arbitration procedures, might leave them better off at the end of the day. The number of areas where this could be accomplished might be small, but it could lead to a significant lessening of industrial tensions.

The government was elected in 1979 on a bogus prospectus concerning public sector pay. In office it has stitched together various ad hoc expedients, often unfair, often arbitrary, never consistent. The result is the present situation of muddle, mess and resentment in the public sector. Given the experience of the last five years, both public servants and the general public would welcome a fairer, more logical and more consistent approach to their problems by government.

There are signs that the public is becoming very sceptical of the government pretending to be whiter than white, preaching the philosophy of non-interference while actually soiling their hands by active intervention, sometimes claiming openly to be holding down wages and at other times pretending that they are not involved. Everyone knows that all governments involve themselves in influencing public sector wage settlements and industrial disputes. They need to be open about it, end the charade of secrecy and the illusion of indifference, and instead devise a fairer way of protecting the legitimate demands of the public who pay for a quality of service and standards from the public sector that is now too often far below that which satisfies public opinion.

CHAPTER FOUR

Macro- and Micro-economic Policy

The traditional advantages of individualism . . . efficiency – the advantages of decentralization and of the play of self-interest . . . [are] even greater, perhaps, than the nineteenth century supposed . . . the best safeguard of the variety of life which . . . is the most powerful instrument to better the future.

John Maynard Keynes,
The General Theory of Employment, Interest and Money, 1936

The central question of economic policy is, and must be recognized to be, how the government can stimulate industry to become more competitive and succeed in domestic and international markets. Our first and overriding goal must be to achieve strong and sustained growth for industrial exports. Our economy cannot shelter behind the brittle walls of protectionism, nor can we rely on the discredited magic of monetary mysticism. The right products delivered at the right time, sold at the right price, produced by properly trained and productive workforces, and vigorously marketed around the world, are the only reliable foundations for economic success and increased employment.

The Chancellor of the Exchequer, Nigel Lawson, in the Mais Lecture on 18 June 1984, billed as a definitive statement of the government's approach to economic policy, gave a thoughtful though somewhat complacent and self-congratulatory analysis of the Conservative record. He stated that the policy approach adopted since 1979 had been 'unequivocally vindicated by events', that 'we are now embarking on the fourth year of a sustained economic recovery'. That would have carried more credibility if he had at least admitted to grievous errors in exchange rate management from 1979 to 1981 and if he had accepted that in every year from 1980 the government had overshot their own sacred PSBR targets by, successively, £0.4bn, £0.9bn, £1bn and £2bn. This despite the Chancellor's strictures on those who consistently argued over the same period that the PSBR targets had been set too tight. It is time that the Chancellor admitted that growth has restarted over the last couple of years precisely because monetary policy has been loosened, although behind a façade of restraint. The government now promises that persistence with the present set of policies will mean higher levels of employment 'in the longer term'. But when is this 'longer term'? Do we have to wait, as Keynes said, until we are all dead? Within a month of the Chancellor's lecture the prospects for a sustained economic recovery had receded somewhat. The fall in July 1984 of the pound to below $1.30 for the first time ever and the 2 per cent increase in bank base rates meant that interest rates rose to their highest level for three years. The resultant effect will be to choke off new investment, reduce growth, and give an upward push to unemployment. The fall in the value of the pound and the much higher mortgage rate will eventually feed through into higher inflation. Against this sombre background, the decline in North Sea oil revenues from 1986 (see pp. 57–9) threatens to provoke, at some unpredictable moment, a major balance of payments crisis, forcing the government into yet more defensive measures – expenditure cuts and interest-rate increases – to keep the pound up and inflation down. Unemployment will rise even further. For the sad truth is that, after levelling off and indeed falling somewhat in the second half of 1983, the number of unemployed has risen through 1984, and is set to go on rising.

The government talks about a sustained economic recovery as though this is something which will simply roll on, generating ever more jobs in its wake. But the truth is that the tremors of 1984 precede the growing slide downwards for the British economy. The peak of a modest recovery may well prove to have been in 1984. The US economy is widely expected to slow down and in 1985, after the Presidential election, action is likely to be taken to reduce the Federal deficit. In the absence of coordinated international economic expansion, this will have a depressing effect on the world economy, and certainly on Britain, since the US remains our

largest single export market. A disappointing feature of the recovery
has been the inability of much of British industry, especially
manufacturing, to take advantage of the increase in domestic
demand since 1982. On present forecasts the level of output at the
end of 1984 will still be 10 per cent below the peak of the last cycle
(1979) and on a level similar to that of the late 1960s. Through
1985 and 1986, the all-too-short-lived upturn in the cycle looks
like turning down for Britain. As growth slows, unemployment
will receive a further upward thrust. The increase in interest
rates, prompted by the continuing weakness of the pound against
the dollar, simply means that the onset of the downturn in the
cycle has been accelerated. The gap between interest rates and the
inflation rate since 1980 – between 5 and 6 per cent – has been
historically high. During the 1960s between 2 and 3 per cent was
the normal gap; the increase is another measure of how tight the
present government's monetary targets have been even though in
practice they have not always been adhered to. Since North Sea oil
now accounts for nearly one quarter of our traded exports, its
decline will be a major source of weakness to the balance of
payments, with export revenues falling by amounts well in excess
of £1bn in some years. The years of transition from an oil economy
to a non-oil economy promise to be years of difficulty and slow
growth.

The Chancellor announced rather grandly in the Mais Lecture
that the proper role of macro- and micro-economic policy was

precisely the opposite of that assigned to it by the conventional post-war
wisdom. It is the conquest of inflation, and not the pursuit of growth and
employment, which should be the objective of macro-economic policy.
And it is the creation of conditions conducive to growth and employment
which should be the objective of micro-economic policy.

The danger of this approach is that it necessitates believing that
everyone else has been wrong in every respect about the way
economic policy should be conducted in the thirty-five years
following the war. That is surely rather a grandiose claim even for
Mr Lawson and Mrs Thatcher. In theory, of course, high unemployment was supposed to cause real wages to fall, so as 'to price labour
back into work'. But over the last five years the major difficulty has
been that the trade unions are still strong enough and the labour

market still so rigid that in Britain, unlike the USA, this has not happened. Real wages have risen 18 per cent in British manufacturing since 1979, and employment has fallen by nearly a quarter. By contrast, real wages have risen by only 3 per cent in the USA, a moderation which has helped to check and then reverse the decline in American manufacturing employment. Real wages are now rising strongly in Britain even though over three million are unemployed. Unless this process is reversed, the continuing surge in real wages will eliminate much of the potential gain in competitiveness arising from recent productivity growth. However, the Chancellor proposed nothing in the Mais Lecture to encourage a slower rise in real wages which, on recent USA examples, would now increase employment in Britain.

Some people point to the United States as an example of the success of old-style Keynesian policies. And it is true that by 1984 rapid growth and a substantial fall in unemployment had been achieved with the help of an expansionary fiscal policy, tax cuts, spending increases and a huge budget deficit. And it had been accomplished without a substantial increase in inflation. The dollar had stayed strong, as a result of high American interest rates, in spite of a growing balance of payments deficit, cutting out the inflation which would normally be generated in these circumstances by a weakening currency.

But we have learnt from painful experience that that type of policy combination simply will not work for Britain. Britain is a much more vulnerable open economy than the relatively closed and self-sufficient US economy. A third of our national income is spent on imports, and if the British government embarked on an indiscriminate spending spree, it would quickly produce a surge in imports and a sliding pound, setting off the inflationary spiral once again.

The government's main economic achievement, and this should not be underestimated, has been, after a surge in inflation in 1980/81 to nearly 20 per cent, to bring it down to 5 per cent in 1984. That gain should not be lightly thrown away. The challenge is to contrive measures capable of encouraging expansion which will not burn themselves out in a blaze of inflation. Since, in our economy, the exchange rate is the principal and certainly the quickest route by which spending increases become translated into price rises, the central problem is how to construct policies which, while encouraging expansion, do not involve a rapid fall in the exchange rate. If this can be done, then, as the American experience has demonstrated, expansion can be maintained and unemployment can fall for a considerable period before inflation picks up again as the limits of capacity are reached.

Fastening on to the central fact that in a small, open economy like ours growth can be sustained without accelerating inflation only so long as the exchange rate, once established at a competitive rate, stays basically stable, we need to construct policies over the medium term which offer real promise of sound sustainable growth and steady falls in unemployment.

The first essential is to work with other countries to develop a coordinated approach to the expansion of our economies. Countries which are trading partners can expand together where one country on its own cannot. If Britain launched a dash for growth, acting alone, imports would be sucked in at such a rate that the pound would crash and the only lasting result would be inflation. But if Britain's trading partners were to expand at the same time, so that the increase in imports associated with faster growth in this country were matched by higher exports abroad, our overseas payments would stay in balance, the pound would not slide, the inflationary spiral would not be ignited.

In circumstances such as these, there was very rapid growth for twenty years after the war, with negligible inflation. Then came the collapse of the Bretton Woods agreement and floating exchange rates, and the cooperative approach to international economic policy was lost. In 1978 at the Bonn summit a set of coordinated expansionary measures was successfully agreed by the participating countries, and although the exercise was aborted by the second oil crisis, and the underlying rate of inflation was probably underestimated, the rationale of Bonn remains valid. There are difficult political problems to be overcome in constructing a complementary set of policies, and the 1984 London summit failed to tackle them, but as the coming downturn increases unemployment all over Europe, attitudes may change and new opportunities to develop new international policies will emerge, particularly at the 1985 summit.

What is needed are decisions to make a series of trade-offs, in which each of the seven summit governments agree to take difficult decisions – which they might prefer to avoid, because of their domestic unpopularity – in return for other governments doing the same, with the cumulative impact of reviving the world economy.

The United States Senate has agreed in 1984 to a set of measures designed to reduce the deficit by $40bn over the next three years. This is much less than is required; it still leaves a deficit of over $100bn in 1986/7. A more ambitious combination of expenditure cuts and tax increases, to raise a further $100bn, needs to be accepted for implementation. Without this, the resultant high interest rates will cripple any world economic recovery. Some reduction in the growth rate of US defence expenditure, which makes a substantial contribution to the US deficit, would be more likely if Europe simultaneously offered to shoulder a larger burden of the cost of Europe's conventional defence. It is important to remember that the 1978 Bonn summit package would never have been politically possible for President Carter if NATO had not decided on a 3 per cent increase in conventional defence spending at the same time. NATO will have to try and assemble a new agreement over defence spending in 1985 to offset the otherwise certain dramatic fall in the defence spending of the European members of NATO in 1986. Such a fall would understandably have a very adverse reaction in Washington.

Europe, too, needs to coordinate a modest reflation, to offset any action in 1985 by the United States to reduce its budget deficit. Germany and Britain should agree to utilize some of their existing spare capacity primarily through such non-inflationary measures as selective capital investment and a reduction in the tax burden on industry. Also, more vigorous measures must be taken on a European scale to encourage the growth of the new technologically based industries, linked to more defence equipment being manufactured and designed in Europe and starting to reverse the present 10:1 imbalance of European military procurement in favour of the US.

Japan must be persuaded to raise its relatively low level of aid to developing countries in 1985. At present Japanese official development assistance to developing countries represents only 0.3 per cent of the GNP. A significant contribution would be $3bn over three years, making up the shortfall in the seventh International

Development Association replenishment. It should also undertake more investment projects in western Europe, supplying both capital and technological expertise; and should take positive steps towards the internationalization of the yen and the liberalization of its financial markets.

All seven summit countries must try to establish, by the time they meet in 1985, a coordinated programme which directs them towards achieving sustained non-inflationary economic growth, raising living standards and bringing down unemployment. Growth of less than 3 per cent for the rest of the decade in the OECD countries as a whole is unlikely to meet these requirements; something closer to 4 per cent ought to be aimed at. The ability of the developing countries to service their debt will depend critically on the growth rate of the western industrialized countries. If the OECD countries grow at around 3.5 per cent per annum between now and 1990, the external debt of the twenty-one main debtor countries will rise from $580bn in 1984 to $820bn in 1990 – a serious situation, but one that should be containable. In addition, the IMF should be provided with the necessary resources – possibly a further $50bn more than the 1983 $100bn agreed quota – to enable it to support debtor countries that need time to service their debts and avoid default.

In addition, policy coordination is essential in the field of exchange rates between the five countries in the Versailles Group to avoid the costs of both the volatility and the misalignment of currencies that have occurred since floating began in 1973. To achieve this Britain must become a full participating member of the European Monetary System (EMS) so that, within the Versailles Group, we can play a full part, with France and Germany, as one leg of a tripod of international currency stability, the others being the yen and the dollar. Britain is particularly vulnerable to international capital movements, far more so than Germany or France, and in particular much more vulnerable to changes in market sentiment. This is why Britain has to show some caution about the way in which we enter the EMS exchange-rate system and why we must not overstress the benefit which will occur. We would need a once-for-all depreciation against the European currencies if we were still uncompetitive at the time of entering the exchange-rate system. Ideally for Britain the dollar should fall from its 1984 height through 1985, the main beneficiary being the Deutschmark. In these circumstances sterling would strengthen against the dollar, which would be good for inflation, and weaken against the European currencies, which would be good for trade. It is important that room is made within the EMS for such a sterling adjustment. Skill would be needed to secure the necessary once-for-all depreciation without undermining confidence and generating expectations of further continuing depreciation; if this could be done we might avoid being obliged to use the wider band adopted by the lira. The other skill needed is to manage the depreciation without unleashing inflationary pressures, and this is where a robust voluntary incomes policy would be required.

Complacency, fatalism and insensitivity have for the last few years predominated in all the international economic forums, the IMF, the World Bank, the OECD and the economic summit meetings. If the summit process fails again in 1985 the world economy will be acutely vulnerable; we will have been ill-served by the very heads of government who ought to have the broader vision and understanding of their responsibilities to provide both national and international leadership.

With or without international action the essential task for Britain is to improve the international competitiveness of our own industry, as the principal means of creating jobs. Expanding our share of export markets and winning the battle against imports is the way to combine expansion and falling unemployment on the one hand, with balance of payments strength, a stable exchange rate and acceptable inflation on the other.

There are three major macro-economic policy initiatives which are necessary to improve competitiveness. First we must make certain that industry has the financial resources to underpin sustained growth. The decline in manufacturing industry's gross investment in recent years has been such that it no longer covers depreciation. Net investment in manufacturing industry has been negative for the past three years; our industrial base is quite simply still running down. On most indicators of cost competitiveness Britain's position is still less favourable than in 1979. If we are to achieve sustained growth we must make certain that more investment is made in new factories to produce new products by radically new production methods. This needs new money. At present industry is faced not only with real interest rates at record levels, but with key money markets which are not working well. In spite of inflation coming down, there has been no spontaneous regeneration in the supply of medium-term fixed-interest money for industry. An industrial credit scheme is needed which would stimulate the supply of fixed-interest money to industry for innovation while leaving the credit risks with the financial institutions. Such a scheme could have a significant impact in improving the flow of funds to industry. For instance, a subsidy of £100m a year over five years could enable £2,000m of five-year medium-term loans to be made available to industry at a rate 5 per cent below the current rate.

Second – we must improve the application of new technology in British industry. If we want to reach the levels of industrial employment and real wages which exist in the richer OECD countries, we must make certain that our industries operate international best-practice techniques and produce more new products. This means – as is argued in much greater detail in Chapter 2 – increasing the funds allocated to industrial R & D and aiming them more specifically at the commercial exploitation of new technology. We should introduce tax incentives to encourage increases in research and development, making the target at least 10 per cent of the OECD total by 1990 compared with 7.5 per cent in 1975. We should also make certain that the proportion of government R & D funds going to industry is increased and directed more specifically at commercial targets.

Third, the government must ensure that there are enough people available with the skills industry needs if it is to succeed in international markets. The most serious deficiency in British industry today is the lack of skills at all levels. For every industry which has failed because of outdated trade union practices, another has failed because management has not adopted best-practice techniques or has not produced new products. We need much more real effort and investment in upgrading the skills of our workforce.

Half the members of the boards of large manufacturing companies in Japan are trained in engineering and science, and in higher technology companies the number lies between 70 and 100 per cent. To meet this challenge we must ensure that our education system is at once less specialized and more technologically orientated than today. Japan produces five times the number of engineers per head of population that we do, and we should aim to reduce this lead substantially over the next ten years.

But Britain's problems will not be solved only in the boardrooms. On the shop floor, where it counts even more, skill shortages are even worse, and may well do much to explain why, in many industries, we have in this country lower productivity per manhour, even in factories using the same capital equipment as that used in other countries. The training at these levels should ideally be done within companies and the introduction of a remissible tax system would encourage firms to make certain that the right level and quality of training is undertaken. Within each industry, perhaps as defined by Minimum List Headings, there is, in any given year, a ratio between training expenditure (not including trainees' salaries) and the total wage bill. Under a remissible tax system, each company which spent *more* than that percentage on training would have all its extra expenditure on training rebated from public funds in the following year. Any company which spent *less* than that percentage would have to pay a tax equal to its underspending. Hence each firm would have a strong tax incentive to increase its training expenditure. The total percentage of the national wage-bill spent on training would be induced to rise year by year but the cost to the Exchequer would be small, since in any year the government would pay only for the cost of any increased expenditure by companies.

Innumerable micro-economic policies are necessary to improve competitiveness. Despite the importance which the government says it attaches to micro-economic or 'supply-side' improvements, its approach to policy over a five-year period has been piecemeal, incoherent and unsatisfactory. The problem is not one of identifying what needs to be done. The list of worthwhile micro-economic reforms is both long and familiar – it is implementing them that is difficult. We have seen in the miners' strike, for example, how difficult it is to reduce the monopoly power of public sector unions.

Trade union reform is a vital part of improving the competitiveness of British industry. For example, industry cannot carry higher energy costs than its competitors. To believe that the mining industry can ignore the cost of continuing grossly uneconomic pits is to continue down the path of economic unreality. In 1972 the

miners' strike had widespread public support and their claim to
have slipped in the industrial league table was justified by Lord
Wilberforce's award of 27 per cent. The mass picketing at Saltley
however was an ominous foretaste of what was to come. By 1973
the miners' action was less popular and less justifiable. It was
politically inept of Mr. Heath to call an election, rather than to
concede under obvious duress and then come back with considered
reforms of the trade unions as part of an election manifesto when
the bitterness of the dispute had settled. After a few months to
reassess the implications of the miners' action the electorate might
have supported serious reform. By the 1979 election, in the
aftermath of the winter of discontent where disruption, picketing
and secondary action reached new heights, the public support for
trade union reform was obvious. Against this background it was
all the more surprising that in the 1984 miners' strike the British
Steel Corporation was not given the go-ahead by the government
to use the civil law when the mass secondary picketing of the
Orgreave coking plant led to incredible scenes of violence. Then the
strike was in its early stages, though sufficiently established for it
to be clear that the 50,000 working miners would continue to
work. Instead, the government relied on a massive police presence
which, because of some unfortunate incidents, although they were
in general well handled, allowed some to infer a wholly false and
damaging equivalence between pickets and police. It is worth
recalling that the government had to be pressured in 1982 by
the SDP to bring forward legislation to reform the democratic
processes of trade unions, bringing their decision-making closer to
the views of their members. The government was unwise in 1984
not to insist on postal ballots, as distinct from workplace ballots,
being the norm rather than the exception. It was as if the government did not understand the purpose of their own legislation. The
use of mass picketing and extensive secondary action, which
gathered momentum after Saltley, made it economically vital that
the balance of power in industrial disputes was redressed so as to
restrict the disruptive power of monopoly trade unions. Trade
union reform is not, therefore, a weapon against trade unionism,
to be judged only in terms of whether it weakens trade unions or
maintains law and order. It should be judged on whether or not it
helps to create a climate of greater commercial realism on the shop

floor of industry and furthers the cause of more democratic, effective and responsible trade unionism.

The government's defence of their reluctance to implement their law reforms relating to secondary picketing is that it was purely tactical. But it is likely that their reluctance will leave the public with the impression that secondary picketing is acceptable and will in future be contained by the police and the criminal law. That will be to enhance, not weaken, public sector labour monopoly power.

A micro-economic measure to reform the social security system to improve incentives has sadly become just another long-term goal, secondary to making short-term savings; in the meantime, the poverty trap increases the disincentives for those on low incomes to return to work. New tax incentives designed to cut the marginal cost of employing extra people, which operate on the real cost of employment as a proxy for the real wage, could make a useful contribution to the micro-economy. By contrast, the government has continued to add to the costs of employing extra people by raising employers' national insurance contributions. Privatization has not, with the exception of the National Freight Corporation, promoted greater competition in the market and more often it has become just another way of raising revenue to offset the rising PSBR. Company tax changes may help capital mobility, but nothing comparable has been done to aid labour mobility, although the introduction of portable pensions would be a useful first step. The government argues toughly that it is essential for people to 'price themselves into work', in effect to accept a drop in real wages if an increase in employment is to be secured; but paradoxically the government has priced people out of work and produced no new labour market measures to cut labour costs. Within a more expansionary macro-economic framework a coherent micro-economic policy is crucial. Over the past twenty years 32 million jobs have been created in the US as against only 4 million jobs in the European Community over a similar period, where the total labour force is larger. The lesson we must learn from the United States is that the credit for the recent fall in unemployment belongs at least partly to much more flexible and market-sensitive institutions and behaviour on the micro-side of the US economy.

A combination of these macro- and micro-economic policies for industrial success, pursued with consistency and determination, could produce for Britain a strong balance of payments position and a buoyant exchange rate. It should, however, be no part of British policy to generate large trade surpluses at the expense of the international community. Instead, inherent balance of payments strength, particularly from the foreign assets acquired during the North Sea oil revenue peak, would enable us to pursue more expansionary domestic policies – with more spending for example on the NHS and on education – without the inflationary consequences which would otherwise appear. This is the application of Keynesianism coinciding with improved competitiveness and it would succeed in this country, providing a vital element in any strategy for jobs.

Extra imports would be covered by a more rapid growth of exports, the stability of the pound would be maintained and, judging from the American experience, inflation could be expected to stay low until the limits of industrial capacity were reached and until signs of strain began to re-emerge in the labour market.

There is a justified fear that inflation might prove a more formidable barrier to expansion than in the United States and rear its head earlier in the process of expansion, before an adequate fall in unemployment had been achieved. This happened in 1971–2 with private-sector-led wage inflation. It could happen again. If it did, the least damaging action would be to impose a counter-inflation tax on inflationary pay settlements to discourage excessive increases and enable growth to continue. The main criticism of the tax – that it would be unfair on the employees of a firm that had accepted restraint for some years but was now profitable and could afford to pay generously, or that it is a tax on success – can be answered by allowing such firms to pay more than the upper range of pay in the national guidelines through the issue of shares which would not be marketable for some years and so would not have immediate inflationary consequences. The critics of an inflation tax have nothing to offer other than what has been tried before: the distortions, rigidities and horse-trading of a trade-union-dominated social contract, or the continuation of indefinite recession and high unemployment. A counter-inflation tax held as a reserve power would testify to a government's determination to hold inflation back and to reduce unemployment. It would give government an independent parliamentary-backed power base which it could probably use as a lever to negotiate a voluntary sustainable agreement between employers and trade unions.

In addition it is psychologically important, with 3 million plus unemployed, more than a million of them under twenty-five, and more than a million unemployed for over a year, that measures are taken which will have an immediate if limited impact in the short term. One imaginative policy would be for employers' national insurance contributions to be abolished for additional employees, so if companies take on extra people they would not be required to pay NI contributions for a specified period. Another would involve a hiring subsidy, payable weekly, for each additional job created, compared with the previous year, which is filled from the young unemployed or the long-term unemployed. Direct cost-effective action of this kind is needed to create the political climate of cooperation and confidence to allow medium-term action to make markets work better and improve long-term competitiveness.

A major change of direction is required to develop an economic policy which offers a combination of macro-economic management and micro-economic liberalism. This means measures to improve competitiveness, supplemented by a stimulus to demand of a more traditional Keynesian kind. In order to avoid unacceptable inflationary consequences, expansion must be kept in step with the extent to which we become competitive. There is an alternative way to achieve competitiveness, despite the government's claims to the contrary; by this method we can prevent unemployment rising steadily from present levels for years to come and start the process of economic recovery and the reversal of Britain's economic decline, hopefully before that decline becomes absolute.

CHAPTER FIVE

Towards
Green Growth

Growth and the environment are not in necessary opposition ... Societies can still 'grow', yet still preserve and enhance their environments.
            Barbara Ward, with René Dubos, *Only One Earth*, 1972

The environment is a bio-political issue of great importance, for its parameters go far beyond the boundaries of national policy. The growth in the world's population is the greatest single factor which can damage the global environment, for the population is estimated to increase by 55 per cent from 4.1 billion people in 1975 to between 6.1 and 6.35 billion by the year 2000, according to the medium-growth projections of the *Global 2000 Report*. While the rate of growth of the world population slowed down in the 1970s and this trend is expected to continue, in absolute terms the increase in population will continue to be bigger in each successive decade. In the more-developed regions population grew by about 0.7 per cent a year over the past decade, and is expected to grow by about 0.6 per cent over the next decade and by 0.5 per cent to the year 2000, but in the less-developed regions population is still growing by about 2 per cent a year, and in Africa by about 3 per cent a year. The less-developed regions' share of the world's population increased from 66 per cent in 1950 to 72 per cent in 1975, and is expected to reach 80 per cent by 2000.

   The last few decades have seen an explosive growth in urbanization, particularly in the developing countries, which in itself has had marked environmental consequences; this trend will continue, but at a slower pace than hitherto. In 1950, 130 million people in developing countries lived in cities of 100,000 or more. By 1975 the figure had risen to 480 million; by the year 2000 it is expected to be over 1 billion. Rapid urban growth puts pressures on sanitation, water supplies, health care, food, shelter and jobs. The developing countries will have to increase urban services by approximately two thirds by 2000 just to stay even with the 1975 levels of service per capita. In the decades ahead, lack of food for the urban poor, lack of jobs and increasing illness and congestion are forecast; these will slow the growth of large cities and modify the still-upward trend of the population but the environmental consequences of rapid growth are likely to continue for many years to come.

The distribution of energy resources will also be critical for the environment. Energy demand has been slowing down since the first oil price shock in the early 1970s but is forecast to rise rapidly towards the end of the 1980s as GDP growth recovers. Beyond this, if GDP in the developed countries grows at nearly 4 per cent a year and at around 5 per cent a year between 1985 and 1995, world energy consumption is forecast to rise by about 2.3 per cent a year in the early 1990s, a lower figure than the 3 per cent growth in the 1970s. This projection assumes further progress in conservation and the production of new energy supplies.

But despite conservation efforts, which will increase and will lead to a small fall in their consumption of oil, the long-term dependence of the developed countries on imported oil will not diminish greatly, since their own production – in the North Sea and elsewhere – is expected to decline gradually. The OPEC countries will thus remain the main exporters of oil and exert a strong influence on international energy prices.

Rising demand for energy will influence the pattern of energy prices. In the short term, prices will continue to fall in response to low demand. A prolonged period of depressed oil prices, and hence energy prices, would slow the pace of energy conservation and limit the production of alternative forms of energy supply. But, as GNP growth starts to recover, real oil prices will rise, and energy demand will grow more quickly than the availability of inexpensive supplies. By the mid 1990s the real price of oil is expected to be about 20 per cent above its peak in 1981.

The future pattern of energy consumption is likely to differ a great deal from that of the oil-dominated 1970s. Oil consumption is forecast to contribute only 11 per cent of the total increase in global energy consumption between 1980 and 1995, compared with 43 per cent between 1970 and 1980. Instead coal, nuclear power and natural gas are expected to compensate for this declining share of oil in the energy consumed in future decades. The developed countries will turn increasingly to coal and nuclear power to meet their energy needs, even though their usage at present is constrained by environmental concerns, high transport costs and safety concerns. Rising project costs have resulted in a sharp reduction of synthetic fuel projects; non-conventional fuels, such as solar power and tidal power, are likely to have only a small role during the late 1980s and early 1990s. Conservation of power is still neglected in energy-investment programmes.

While prices for oil and other commercial energy sources are rising, fuelwood – the 'poor country's oil' – is forecast to become far less available than it has been in the 1970s. The demand for fuelwood in the developing countries is estimated to increase by 2.2 per cent a year between 1984 and 1994, as opposed to an annual rate of growth of 1.8 per cent a year between 1974 and 1984. This increase in demand will lead to local fuelwood shortages in 1994 totalling 650 million cubic metres – about a quarter of the projected need. This implies that fuel consumption for essential uses will be reduced, deforestation increased, wood prices increased, and growing amounts of crop residues and dung re-allocated from the field to the cooking fire. This could have the most devastating effects on those countries' environment and should be taken into account by the industrialized countries and in our own British environmental energy debate. With finite energy resources, we cannot justify continuing to burn oil in our power stations or abandoning an ongoing nuclear power programme – a source of energy that the developing countries are unlikely to be able to develop for many decades.

In Britain, anxieties about nuclear power have been to a considerable extent assuaged by the Report of the Royal Commission on Environmental Pollution and, in particular, by the Commission's probing of the transport and storage arrangements for plutonium, which has led to a considerable tightening of the controls and safeguards. There is still controversy over whether we should change to a pressurized water reactor (PWR) design. The

British Nuclear Fuels plant at Sellafield/Windscale, a plutonium production reactor, has had a troubled history and is now the focus of justified environmental concern. Over the past few years there have been a series of worrying incidents: the blow-back in 1973 which led to the contamination of thirty-seven workers, the leaking silos discovered in 1976, the near explosion of hydrogen in 1978, the release of radioactive iodine in 1981 and the release which led to the closure of a beach in 1983. Sellafield/Windscale is essential to the nuclear industry, but public confidence is essential if Sellafield/Windscale is to remain open. This record of unfortunate incidents has, however, weakened that confidence. It is important to remember that the long-running Sellafield/Windscale inquiry dealt only with the THORP (thermal oxide reprocessing) plant, which has yet to be built. The worrying possibility of a link with leukaemia only underlines the need for a single authoritative independent investigation.

We know from opinion polls in Britain and elsewhere in the industrial democracies that public interest and concern for the environment is continuously increasing and has not been overtaken or weakened by fears aroused by the recession. The 3 million members of environmental bodies in this country are proof enough of the importance British people attach to their quality of life. There has been a turnaround in values which is not as yet reflected in the values which dominate the political debate.

The establishment of the standing Royal Commission on Environmental Pollution by the Labour government in 1970 was meant to signal the importance of a problem requiring particularly serious attention and to ensure that it was continuously monitored. Since 1970 this Commission has produced nine reports. They have covered many subjects, including nuclear power, agriculture and, most recently, lead. The thoroughness and authority of these reports has earned them respect and influence with many governments throughout the world.

Nevertheless, of the some 300 recommendations made in these reports, only a handful have ever been implemented. Delaying and diversionary tactics have been the norm. In January 1976, for example, the Royal Commission submitted its fifth report, on air pollution, to a Labour government which then had three years to run. In December 1982, a mere six years later, a Conservative government in its third year in office finally replied. It rejected the principal recommendations.

Neither the seventh report, on agriculture, nor the eighth, on oil pollution, dating from 1979 and 1981, has yet received a response from government. Only the ninth report, with its principal recommendation on lead, has been accepted – within one hour of publication. The proximity of the general election concentrated the government's mind since, largely as a result of brilliant campaigning, all the other political parties had openly accepted the banning of lead in petrol.

The history of the Control of Pollution Act is, if possible, an even more damning indictment of the record of successive governments. Enacted by the Labour government in 1974, it has never been fully implemented. A decade later, some of the sections on waste disposal have still not come into force and the timetable for dealing with water pollution stretches out until 1988.

Often, it has only been when European legislation forced the issue that anything has been done at all, but even here the British government delays European efforts to introduce environmental impact assessments, thwarts international efforts to control acid rain and weakens energy conservation. The government allows capital investment in the water and sewerage systems to fall to dangerously low levels. It abolishes the Waste Management Advisory Council and the Noise Advisory Council. It cuts environmental research, factory inspectors and environmental health officers, and attempts to relax planning controls in a way which will release a tide of urban sprawl. All this is accompanied by public assertions if necessary about their concern for the environment.

There are many urgent issues on which the British government could act: the need for money and staff to give proper effect to the Wildlife and Countryside Act following the careful report from Wildlife Link; the need to bring the levels of radioactive discharges from Windscale down to near zero; the need to take action on coal-fired power stations to reduce sulphur and nitrogen oxides in the atmosphere in view of the international concern over acid rain which is polluting lakes in Scotland and Wales, as well as forests in western Europe and Scandinavia; the need for faster action to reduce levels of toxic chemicals such as asbestos and pesticides in the environment. The process by which the government receives advice should be open to much wider participation.

The interests of the agricultural industry have to be balanced against the interests of the countryside; the growing resemblance of parts of rural England to the plains and prairies of North America is deeply resented by a great many people. The destruction of the countryside and its wildlife habitats is not just an aesthetic loss – East Anglia's wildlife and countryside, and the tourism it generates on the Broads, the coast and at its nature reserves, are as important economically as its farming. The same can be said of other rural areas in the UK. While efficient and productive farming must be supported, conservation must not be neglected.

In 1983 the government put forward proposals to relax the regulations protecting the Green Belts and green-field sites; the threat has been averted, but probably only temporarily. Wrong choices here will haunt us for decades to come. Minor changes of practice to give a degree of flexibility in planning might be helpful, but there can be no justification whatsoever for making it easier to build new houses on green-field sites when so much of our existing housing is in need of urgent repair – the neglect of our big cities continues virtually unabated. Ten of the largest private house-builders have formed a consortium hoping to build new private-venture settlements in the countryside around London; this could divert resources from London and from those living in the million houses that are unfit for human habitation or the 7 million houses requiring repairs costing over a thousand pounds. Laisser-faire planning is not the answer to the problems of the 1990s, any more than it was to the situation in the 1920s and 1930s, when the flight from the cities led to urban sprawl and the despoiling of the countryside. That was halted by the start of Green Belt planning and the legislation of 1947 that has made Britain's planning policy admired throughout the world from Los Angeles and São Paulo to Tokyo and Beijing. We in Britain should be stimulating, as in the United States, a 'Back to the Cities' movement. The government's own Housing Condition Survey estimates an essential repairs bill of £30bn for the nation's housing stock, and yet it ignores this and diverts precious housing funds to increasing the rural sprawl. Effort and resources should be concentrated on reversing the flight from the inner cities, not on encouraging it by deepening their physical decay, hastening the drift away of their people and stimulating unbalanced and artificial dormitory development. What is needed are imaginative, inner-city public/private partnerships – partnerships that will produce profits for the builders, certainly, but also benefits for the people. We need real communities with space, gardens and leisure facilities in the cities – restoring the urban environment, not ravaging the rural environment. Of course, we cannot deal simply with the built environment. To improve the lives of those in decaying inner-city areas, we also need to think about the quality of life in terms of jobs, health provision and much else. The planner can inadvertently contribute to the development of a class-ridden society, with the better-off fleeing to the green fields and the disadvantaged abandoned to inner-city ghettos. In all Britain's major metropolitan centres the message is the same – the land is available but the money is missing. The need and the wish for real homes is present, but the political will and the commercial drive cannot be harnessed together to build them. Without a new partnership the private sector will continue to see most profit in building on virgin greenfield sites and will only build low-standard housing in the cities – the high price of the land and other costs would make anything else inordinately expensive.

Winning the battle for the environment is not, however, simply a question of winning isolated skirmishes on this issue or that issue. The central concern of the World Conservation Strategy, the basic problem which links all the disparate issues, is the relationship between the environment and the economy; we must find a sensible balance between these two if we are to create a society which is both ecologically and economically sustainable.

Previous approaches to the environment have assumed that there is an inevitable antithesis between the environment and the economy, that the one can only thrive at the expense of the other. In rejecting this assumption one should expose the fake choice it poses between the further extension of bureaucratic controls or the unchecked assaults of the marketplace. An equally false choice is that between 'growth' and 'no growth'. It is as much of a nonsense to suggest there is an absolute correlation between economic growth and environmental harm as it is to suggest it between economic growth and energy use. What determines the relationship, in both cases, is the kind of growth. We need to develop a thoughtful growth – a green growth that recognizes the interdependence of economic and ecological priorities. The environment provides the context within which all economic activity takes place. It is often forgotten how dependent industrial economies remain on resources that are biological in origin – food, wood, fibres, oils, chemicals and drugs to name but some. Damage to the environment always manifests itself eventually as damage to the economy, whether as lower crop yields, shorter building lifetimes, higher burdens on the health service or rising real-resource costs. Equally, weak and inefficient economies are rarely able to avoid wasting their resources, biological as well as human. Nor are they able to make the economic investments necessary to sustain biological productivity. An economy that is unable to feed and house its population, to keep it warm and healthy and to meet its basic needs for education and personal fulfilment will be in no position to invest in maintaining the integrity of its environment. We have only to look at the places in the Third World suffering the worst environmental degradation to discover they are also the places where poverty is at its most desperate. The most immediate problems facing Britain are those of reducing unemployment and encouraging industrial regeneration and economic recovery. Within the political orthodoxies of class politics this can only be done by sacrificing the environment. In rejecting such orthodox class politics one is also saying that one is not prepared to sacrifice one's children's future in order to preserve one's own. In the environment, as in so many other areas, artificial polarization – competitiveness or compassion, efficiency or equity, growth or no growth, left or right – is irrelevant to reality. What is needed is a new dualism, a synthesis, a combination of what are too often wrongly assumed to be incompatible objectives. It is not easy to achieve, but it is possible to develop a programme which balances economic and ecological imperatives, reduces environmental damage and contributes to economic recovery.

The environment should not be a fringe issue for politicians, to be considered as an afterthought, a hastily included 'green' gloss on an otherwise grey manifesto. It is necessary to bring the environment closer to the heart of economic policy so as to achieve a balance between economy and ecology. A well-designed public-investment programme could achieve more jobs in Britain, and each of the specific projects in such a programme – energy conservation, repair and renewal of the water and sewerage system, improvements in bus and rail services, housing rehabilitation, bypass construction, rail electrification and better telecommunications – would bring with it significant environmental gains. Every one of these proposals has featured high on the agenda of environmental organizations in this country. We also need an environmental improvement programme aimed at creating jobs on environmentally vital tasks such as tree-planting and derelict land reclamation.

Another challenge is to shift the emphasis in environmental policy away from the merely reactive and curative towards measures which are anticipative and preventative. This necessarily involves a shift from a predominant use of regulative and regulatory mechanisms to ones in which investment decisions, taxation policy, grants and other financial incentives play an increasing role. Such an approach also involves a greater degree of interaction between environment policy and other key policy areas including agriculture, energy and transport. This would place more emphasis on opportunities than constraints. Farmers, industrialists and others involved in economic activity should not only be prevented from damaging the environment, they must also be encouraged to improve it. Industry would respond to incentives to firms to adopt cleaner and more resource-efficient technologies and to train advertising, marketing and design personnel to identify environmentally benign products and markets. In agriculture, more job-creation funds should be available for projects in agriculture where labour is required to bolster conservation, with the Ministry of Agriculture re-ordering its grants priorities to encourage environmentally appropriate practices. As reform of the European Common Agricultural policy proceeds, considerable strains will be put on rural communities and it will require sensitive handling for its economic and environmental consequences.

British agriculture is, however, capable of adaptation, as it has shown over the last ten years. It has almost doubled its volume of food exports to the European Community since joining, and quadrupled their value, from £650m to £2.5bn; in the same period our food imports have remained practically static. The balance of trade has thus benefited substantially. In cereals in 1973/4 we imported 1.7 million tonnes from EEC countries; in 1983/4 we exported 1 million tonnes to those same countries.

We hear a great deal about the butter mountain, but much less about our butter exports. Dutch and French butter has become familiar in our shops, but not as familiar as our butter in their shops. We sell them 2.5 kilos of butter for every kilo they sell us. Britain gains nothing from distorting the true record of the Community in agriculture or making mean-spirited demands without attempting to understand their impact on the rural economies and environment of our European partners.

What matters is to get on with the job of eliminating surplus food production. More realistic production targets can be set, quotas can be extended, though in a planned and fair way which protects vulnerable rural communities in economic and environmental terms. National quotas should be angled to buttress regional policy and take account of social or environmental problems as they affect the agricultural industry, in the way that we consider normal for other industries.

Care and concern for the environment is frequently linked to a commitment to a more decentralized society, for although there is a powerful role for central government, most of the decisions that cumulatively make an environmental impact are taken locally. As we move ever more quickly towards a centralized state, crushing the individual's identification with parish and ward, and reorganize local government in a way that ensures that planning is divorced from the community and the citizen, we are daily threatening the quality of life of the generations to come. This piecemeal destruction of the environment will continue until we develop a new political consensus which is more biologically sensitive and more attuned to the views of communities. Environmentalists are but one of the groups within our society yearning for the development of a more representative democracy.

CHAPTER SIX

Responsibilities
to the Unemployed

A host of unemployed citizens face the grim problem of existence – only a foolish optimist can deny the dark realities of the moment ... where there is no vision the people perish.
President Franklin D. Roosevelt, First Inaugural Address, March 1933

The most serious social and political problem facing Britain at the present time is the rise in the level of unemployment. Yet there is an all-pervading sense of fatalism about its continuance. We have become conditioned to accept or tolerate it because it has crept up on us by degrees. It has dampened our indignation. It is hard to remember that when, in 1962, unemployment rose to what by present standards is an extremely low number – 350,000 (1.7 per cent), the political storm was such that Harold Macmillan, the then Prime Minister, sent Quintin Hogg, Lord Hailsham as he is now, to the north-east, donning a cloth cap in the process, to demonstrate the Conservative government's concern. In 1972 Edward Heath did his famous U-turn on economic policy when unemployment had reached 3.7 per cent. In 1979 when James Callaghan's Labour government left office unemployment was 5.2 per cent. But by the middle of 1984, on the same basis of comparison, it was 12.9 per cent. Public opinion has been lulled into complacency by the constant reiteration of the statement that this is a world problem. In many senses this is true and solutions have to be sought internationally as well as within Britain. Nevertheless, the British level of unemployment is higher than in most other comparable countries. In 1970 in the western democratic OECD countries the unemployment rate was 3 per cent. It rose to a little over 5 per cent in the mid-1970s, in the wake of the first oil shock, and then stabilized. But since the beginning of 1980 it has climbed dramatically. By 1984 the rate was around 10 per cent, representing some 35 million people. Experience has, however, differed between countries. In North America unemployment peaked at about 8.5 per cent in 1975, fell to around 6 per cent in 1979, and then rose sharply. But it peaked again, at about 11 per cent, at the end of 1982, and since then has been falling. In western Europe, by contrast, there was no fall in unemployment during the mid-1970s, and the renewed rise since early 1980, which has brought it to over 10 per cent, shows no signs of going into reverse. In Japan, unemployment remains very low by the standards of other countries – though this partly reflects different techniques of measurement; even so, at around 2.5–3 per cent, it is twice as high as a decade ago.

Different groups have been affected differently by the rise in unemployment. Male unemployment has risen in the OECD countries much faster than female unemployment since 1980, reflecting both a slowing down in the growth of the female labour force, and the particularly severe effect of the recession on the mining, manufacturing and construction sectors, where male employment is high relative to female employment. Young people have been hit particularly hard, with nearly one in five of those under twenty-five being without a job. In Japan the figure is relatively low – though still, at around 5 per cent, nearly twice the national unemployment rate. In the United States the figure is about 17 per cent, though among disadvantaged groups, particularly young blacks and Hispanics in the big cities, the figures are far higher. In a number of western European countries the youth-unemployment rate is well over 20 per cent, with much higher figures among ethnic minorities in particular areas. A further feature of the present unemployment problem is the rise in long-term unemployment, particularly in western Europe, where more than a third of those who are unemployed have been unemployed for a year or more.

Some observers have seen in the sharp rise in unemployment in recent years the operation of deep-seated and elusive forces at work in the world economy, as described by the Kondratieff or long-wave theory of fifty-year cycles of economic development: the deep recessions of the 1880s, the 1930s and now the 1980s, they argue, exhibit too great a regularity to be accidental. But no satisfactory explanation of why there should be such a regularity has been advanced, and the fact that only three observations of the phenomenon so far exist must make the data statistically suspect. Much more concrete explanations of the recent rise in unemployment can be pointed to.

One of these is the fact that, particularly since the mid-1970s, the population of working age has been rising faster than the total population. The relationship between this phenomenon and the rise in unemployment is a complex one. In the EEC, where the labour force grew relatively slowly, unemployment grew fastest because there was an actual fall of 3 million in total employment between 1973 and 1983. In the US, by contrast, a rapidly growing labour force and a marked rise in female participation rates were accompanied by the creation of 13 million new jobs over the same period. Nevertheless, a rise in the proportion of the population which is of working age, a demographic feature which would have helped to raise living standards if the demand for labour had been high, has contributed to swelling the ranks of the unemployed at a time when the demand for labour has been low.

A much more significant factor behind the rise in unemployment, particularly in western Europe, has been structural shifts in the demand for labour. Some of this has reflected the microelectronic revolution and the significant savings of labour which the widespread adoption of the microprocessor is making possible in many manufacturing and service industries. This has been discussed in Chapter 2, on the high-tech revolution. What is worth stressing here is that while rapid and widespread adoption of microelectronic technology is in one sense merely the latest instalment in the kind of technological change that has been at work raising productivity and living standards over the past two centuries, it is, in other ways, however, very different. One factor which is different is the speed with which the new technology has been developed and disseminated. The first integrated circuit was produced for military purposes in 1958, but it was only in the later 1960s that price falls led to a significant spread of the technology beyond the military field. The microprocessor – the central processing unit of a computer, contained on a chip – was first developed only in 1971. Yet by the end of the 1970s micro-electronic technology had created new products and led to new techniques of production on a significant scale – a process which is rapidly continuing. Moreover, the technology itself is changing at breakneck speed: late in 1983, for example, one firm launched a new microprocessor chip which is said to be able to compute at 10 million instructions a second – as fast as the largest IBM computer of only three years earlier.

The microelectronic revolution has yielded, and will continue to yield, enormous benefits. One is a range of new products, ranging from consumer goods like video tape-recorders, pocket calculators and electronic watches to services of various kinds, such as electronic transfers of funds and mass air travel. Another benefit is new processes of production, which permit goods to be produced very much more cheaply. More output, permitting higher consumption of new and better goods, produced with less labour – this can reasonably be regarded as constituting the kind of rise in living standards which is the ultimate objective of economic policy. But there is another side to the coin: the speed and scale of the microelectronic revolution has begun to involve significant displacement of labour. People who lose their jobs – or fail to find them in the first place – because a computer or robot can do the job better may find it easier to see the costs of the process than the benefits.

Displacement of labour has been particularly marked in manu-facturing industry as, for example, robots replace men in car-assembly plants; and where the operations of banks and insurance companies have become increasingly computerized, reducing the need for certain types of clerical labour. Some of the new products have a treble effect in displacing labour: electronic typewriters or word processors, for example, are much cheaper to produce than electro-mechanical typewriters, because they contain fewer com-ponents to manufacture and assemble; they significantly increase the productivity of secretaries and typists; and, having few moving parts, need less repair and maintenance. In consequence, the demand for three different kinds of labour has been reduced.

The reduction in the demand for many kinds of labour is, of course, only part of the picture: there is rising demand for other kinds of labour. In some cases one type of skilled labour is replaced by another; for example, the linkages being established between numerically controlled machine tools and computer-aided design reduce the demand for draughtsmen, precision engineers and tool-setters, but increase the demand for systems analysts and computer programmers. In the typical case it is semi-skilled and unskilled labour which is displaced by the new technologies; the jobs created require skills and qualifications.

The overall effect that microelectronics will have on employment and unemployment over the next decade or so is a matter of dispute. Some of the studies which have been conducted come to the pessimistic conclusion that the job losses which occur will not be compensated by much employment creation elsewhere. The majority of studies are more optimistic, concluding that compensation will be somewhere between 50 and 100 per cent; and a few take the view that it may be over 100 per cent. For present purposes, however, there are two specific views which are of particular importance.

The first is the virtually unanimous view among those who have studied the matter that far more jobs will be lost by countries which lag behind in the introduction of the new microelectronic technologies than by those which are in the vanguard of this process; indeed much of the difference in the estimates of compensation derives from different assumptions about the relative pace of introduction of these technologies in particular countries.

The second view, widely held, is that Europe is already beginning to lag badly behind the US and Japan in the speed and scale of its adjustment to the microelectronic era. But this is an oversimplified way of depicting the real situation. Although containing certain aspects of truth, such an assessment hides a far more complex state of affairs. There are certain sectors in which Europe as a whole is in the forefront of technical advance. These include nuclear energy and all the technologies connected with the nuclear fuel cycle; biotechnology, especially where the food and pharmaceutical industries are involved; even robotics and numerically controlled machines, mainly where high-precision or high-flexibility instrumentation is required; and professional electronics, especially when applied to the public service sector, including postal delivery, transportation and telecommunication systems. The other area of European strength is a proven ability to inject emerging technologies, such as lasers and microprocessors, into traditional industrial fields. This integration of new technologies and traditional sectors has allowed the revamping and rationalization of mature industries like textiles, which only a few years ago seemed condemned to migration to the Third World.

The relative weakness of Europe compared to the United States and to Japan is due to its low standing in a variety of solid-state technologies: Very Large Scale Integrated Circuits and semiconductors – such as the 'silicon chip' – advanced electronic components and circuits, and the development of large-scale computers are not areas where Europe has been able to compete. This is an ominous trend for Europe and clearly much must be done if the problem – in these sectors at least – is not to continue to worsen.

The effects of the new microelectronic technology have been building up for little more than a decade, but they have been building up fast, and perhaps at an accelerating pace. Some of their impact on people's lives, both as producers and consumers, has already been felt, but much more is still to come. Handled properly, the new technology can confer great benefits not only on countries where it has mainly been developed and adopted, but on the world as a whole. But there can be no confidence as yet that the large-scale displacement of labour that the new technology is bringing in its train can be successfully turned into greater leisure for all rather than permanent enforced idleness for those who are directly affected.

Another factor in the rise in unemployment reflects changing comparative advantage: not only Japan, but many of the newly-industrializing countries as well, have become more efficient than western Europe and part of North America at producing goods – textiles, clothing, footwear, steel, ships and a number of other products – which until relatively recently have constituted the bedrock output of the older industrial areas. In general, again particularly in western Europe, resources have been slow to move out of these old industries into new ones; and although rising demand for both public and private services has led to an expansion of employment in the services sector, much of this extra employment has been provided by women not previously in the labour force, and has thus failed to lead to a corresponding fall in unemployment.

The major reason for the sharp rise in unemployment in recent years undoubtedly lies in the macro-economic policies which the main industrialized countries have been pursuing. The rise in the inflation rate in the late 1960s and early 1970s, the further boost to world inflation given by the first oil shock of 1973–4, the plunge into balance of payments deficits of most of the main industrial countries, and the fear of further inflationary and balance of payments problems after the second oil shock in 1979–80, all combined to promote restrictive macro-economic policies in these countries, particularly after 1979. These policies have been successful in the sense that the OECD inflation rate has been brought down from around 12 per cent in 1980 to 6 per cent in 1983, and to an even lower rate in most of the OECD countries. But the other side of the coin was that between 1979 and 1983 total OECD output grew, on average, by little more than 1 per cent a year – much more slowly than the underlying growth in productivity. The resulting fall in the demand for labour has obviously been a prime factor in the rise in unemployment.

A high incidence of short-term unemployment is not necessarily to be deplored; it may be a reflection of a society adapting rapidly to change. But the contemporary phenomenon – particularly in western Europe – of a high rate of long-term unemployment, which represents prolonged periods of joblessness for a minority of the labour force, is particularly damaging. It conflicts with the work ethic which underlies the growth in prosperity in the western democracies over the past century, according to which able-bodied citizens must contribute to the creation of this prosperity if they are to enjoy its fruits. For those who suffer involuntary unemployment, such a contribution is rendered impossible; the basis on which society is organized is correspondingly weakened. The marked increases in labour productivity being made possible by the microelectronic revolution call, over the next decade, for completely new thinking about the relationships between work, income and leisure. The hallmark of democratic governments worldwide cannot be a fatalistic acceptance of the permanent unemployment of a large and possibly growing proportion of their labour force.

Two of the groups which suffer from long-term unemployment are of particular concern. One is the middle-aged – particularly men – who lose their jobs because their firm closes down or their skills are made obsolete by technical progress. Some of these people take advantage of their enforced leisure, developing new skills and interests, but others suffer a loss of self-respect, become apathetic or depressed, and lose interest in life. Even more serious is the plight of the other group – the youthful unemployed. Young people who on leaving school or after higher education search in vain for a job for months, which can stretch into years, are likely to feel – and with some justice – that they have been rejected by society. That some of them should take refuge in alcohol or drugs or crime is hardly surprising; but it is a searing indictment of the failure by the societies in which they have grown up to provide them with a fundamental human right: the right to work. It is no use extolling the merit of democracy on the one hand while on the other ignoring this social evil that has once again, as in the twenties and thirties, returned to prey on the conscience of democracies.

Undue alarmism may well be out of place; but so is undue complacency. It does not seem particularly fanciful to discern, in high rates of long-term unemployment among the young, the seeds of a threat to our democratic system. This is particularly true of western Europe, where youth unemployment rates of well over 20 per cent are already common, and where, on present trends, the problem is going to get worse. On the other side of the ideological divide, in east Europe, there appears, by contrast, to be no great unemployment problem. But to a generation of young people in western Europe facing the prospect of an indefinite period of unemployment and a standard of living no higher than that provided by social security benefits, the relative attractions of the democratic and communist systems could come to assume a different perspective. It is easy for well-informed observers to point to the gross inefficiencies and high level of disguised unemployment in the Soviet system, and to argue that one of the Soviet Union's methods of preventing overt unemployment is to force millions of people to work in uncongenial jobs and in unpleasant places like Siberia. But already the claim that parliamentary democracy is incapable of solving our economic and social problems is increasingly being heard in Europe. Nor can we in the industrialized democracies dismiss unemployment in the developing world. Here, too, its recent rapid growth, admittedly from a higher initial base, gives grounds for concern. Many of these countries favour some form of non-alignment, preferring not to choose between the ideologies of communism or capitalism; but even the choice of non-alignment is not fixed. The Soviets certainly pursue in these countries their version of the 'ideological struggle' and we in the West cannot be indifferent to any ideological shift towards communism, particularly where it carries with it security implications.

A crucial feature of any programme for reducing the level of unemployment in Britain and in the OECD countries must be the resumption of a faster rate of economic growth than has been achieved in recent years. Effective demand must be expanded steadily, and methods of dealing with inflation must be devised which do not rely on the kind of severely restrictive fiscal and monetary policies which have been the norm in recent years. But increasing effective demand will not, by itself, be nearly enough; active measures will need to be taken, on a widespread and sustained basis, to ensure that the labour force has the required skills to meet the demand, and is available at the right place and time.

The role of governments in this process is likely to differ. In the United States there is a long tradition of a high degree of labour mobility, in two different senses. Workers have shown considerable willingness to acquire new skills and qualifications, in order to better themselves and increase their earning power; and the geographical mobility of American families – the readiness to move long distances to new locations, as seen in the drift to the south and south-west in the pursuit of better jobs – is of an order quite unfamiliar in Europe where there is an expectation, not in itself unreasonable, but sometimes over-pitched, that governments will bring jobs to deprived regions. American trade unions, moreover, have traditionally welcomed and contributed to the process of technological change, taking the view that this process is the key to higher living standards, at any rate for those who manage to adapt to these changes and to keep their jobs.

An encouraging trend is the shift to service industries as part of the natural evolution of western industrial societies, for it offers scope for absorbing large numbers of unemployed. In the US, for example, nearly all the increase of 13 million jobs between 1973 and 1983 was in three main service areas: wholesale and retail trading; finance, insurance and real estate; and professional, scientific and miscellaneous services. Compared to some European countries, especially Britain, a much higher proportion of the increase in the demand for services fed straight through into an increase in employment.

The position in Europe is, in important respects, different. For various reasons – its older industrial tradition, its larger trade union membership, the pervasive sense of a society with its roots still deep in the past, or the attitudes bred by the destruction wrought by two world wars fought over its soil within the lifetime of its older inhabitants – the resistance to change is greater. By comparison with the United States and Japan, labour markets are relatively inflexible. Workers are less willing to accept technological change, less willing to be retrained for new jobs and less willing to move in search of employment. The degree of inflexibility does indeed vary substantially within Europe – it is considerably greater in Britain than in Germany. There is in Europe a tendency for governments to provide subsidies to keep older and increasingly uncompetitive industries in business, rather than to use the money to alleviate the costs of adaptation to the changing pattern of comparative advantage. This process is justified on the basis that it is better to have people producing goods which are strictly uncompetitive in world markets than to have people producing nothing at all. But too often assistance which is devised in order to cushion the process of change in the short term becomes institutionalized into a system of subsidies in the long term; and the result of this can only be an increasingly arthritic industrial structure, increasingly unable to adapt to new developments or to pay its way in a rapidly changing world.

One suggestion which has been discussed in Europe to improve the workings of the labour market is to cut the level of unemployment benefits, on the supposition that many people find it more agreeable to live on state benefit than to work. But surveys in a number of European countries suggest that this is no more than a marginal problem, and that by far the greatest part of unemployment is genuinely involuntary. Increasingly, therefore, solutions are being sought in ways of making labour markets more flexible, encouraging workers without skills, or with skills that have been rendered obsolete by technical progress, to be trained or retrained.

Although it will sometimes pay private employers to do this, the ultimate responsibility for stimulating the extensive training and retraining that is necessary lies with the state. It is society as a whole that benefits from the higher living standards made possible by technical progress, and it is society as a whole – rather than the individuals directly affected – which must bear the costs of adapting to such change. More vocational training for the young, and a system of retraining for adults whose skills are overtaken by changing job requirements, must come to be regarded as essential obligations of government if the problem of structural unemployment is to be overcome.

The potential increases in productivity stemming from the microelectronic revolution make it unlikely that even sustained economic growth and active labour-market policies will, by themselves, solve the unemployment problem if work continues to be governed by present custom and practice in terms of the hours worked in a week, the weeks worked in a year and the age of retirement. What is needed now is some new thinking about the relationship between hours worked and leisure enjoyed. What must be changed is a situation in which a majority of the population – though a shrinking one – works traditional hours for a traditional working lifetime, while a minority of the population – though an increasing one – does not work at all. Instead, the aim should be to devise arrangements which offer some opportunity for work, and more opportunities for leisure, to all. Ideally arrangements should permit the maximum possible freedom for individuals to choose their own preferred combination of work and leisure. But it may be that such a degree of freedom – which would itself require a change in attitudes on the part of governments, employers and unions – would not result in a move towards work-sharing on the scale required to deal with the unemployment problem. In that event, further action would need to be considered.

The elements of any new arrangements are relatively easy to identify. One is likely to be a longer period of compulsory education or broad vocational training for the young – something needed in any case as part of a more active labour market policy. Another would be a shorter working week, or longer annual holidays, or some combination of the two. Another would be a general lowering of the age of retirement. Another, and particularly important, part of the answer is likely to be a move towards much more extensive job-sharing or part-time working. Important sections of the labour force, such as married women and older workers nearing retirement, are likely to welcome greater opportunities than are generally available at present to work on a part-time basis, rather than working full-time or not at all. The expansion of job opportunities in the service sector should in principle make this desire easier to satisfy. However, the fact that such elements of a solution as these may be relatively easy to discern does not necessarily mean that the solution will be simple to achieve. Two difficulties in particular must be faced.

The first is the possibility that any major move towards work-sharing – with more people at work, but most of them working shorter hours – may confront employers with a significant rise in unit costs; this problem may be especially acute where what is at issue is a shift to a shorter working week or longer paid annual holidays. A rise in unit costs can lead to an erosion of profit margins or an upward twist to inflation, and – if exchange rates are sticky – to a decline in international competitiveness. Nevertheless, the risk of a significant rise in unit costs can be exaggerated. The underlying rationale of the need to reduce working hours if a high level of employment is to be restored and maintained is that the microelectronic revolution makes possible a large increase in the amount produced per working hour, so that the increase in labour costs per hour – assuming that employees work fewer hours per year for the same money – may be offset by rising productivity. Thus unit costs – costs per unit of output – will be stable or perhaps falling. Of course it will not always be the case that the rise in productivity permitted by the microchip and other technological developments will be sufficient to allow for reductions in working hours at unchanged wages. This is most obvious in the case of people who choose to move from full-time jobs to part-time jobs, who would naturally not expect to earn the same amount of money: they have opted for much less income and much more leisure. Moreover, there is bound to be a continuing struggle over the distribution of the fruits of the higher productivity resulting from the microelectronic revolution – a struggle between workers, who want more income for fewer hours, employers, who want higher profits, and consumers, who want lower prices. What is being suggested here is that the workers' share of rising prosperity should take the form not of a rapidly rising income but no increase in leisure for some, but rather of a much slower rise in income and a significant increase in leisure for all. Providing that the increase in leisure is matched to increasing productivity, there is no reason why these changes should result in any increase in inflationary pressures or – in an era of flexible exchange rates – in any reduction of international competitiveness.

A second difficulty that may arise in implementing a strategy of work-sharing and increased leisure as part of the answer to high unemployment is that some of those who have secure jobs may insist on receiving more income rather than more leisure; in other words may seek to grab more than their fair share of the work that is going.

It is difficult to know how far this will really prove a problem. It is true that some groups of workers resist cuts in weekly hours of work – or, if hours are cut, resort to moonlighting rather than enjoy the extra leisure. But the same groups of workers often welcome longer annual holidays or earlier retirement, so reduction in lifetime hours of work could be achieved by a different route. The history of the past hundred years is one of higher living standards in the industrialized countries taking the form of both higher incomes and more leisure, and there is no particular reason why this pattern should change in the future.

Nevertheless, the sheer speed of contemporary technological change raises the distinct possibility that the pace at which workers or employers may wish of their own accord to reduce lifetime hours of work may not be nearly rapid enough to provide job opportunities for the unemployed. If this is so, governments in the industrial countries will have to take the lead – though the form this lead will take will obviously vary according to the nature of the problem in each country and the attitude of its people.

There is much that the British government could do, without resorting to draconian measures such as imposing limits on the amount of work that can be done by individuals or family units. Taxation and social security systems could be adjusted, for example, so as to make part-time employment more attractive to both employer and employee. The financial penalties resulting from early retirement could also be reduced by appropriate tax and benefit provisions. More specifically, where a firm agrees to replace an older worker by a young unemployed worker, the pension or redundancy payments incurred by the firm could in part be financed by the government, which would be offset by the saving on unemployment benefit to the younger worker. However, although the British government should give a lead, by fostering a climate of opinion favourable to a shorter working lifetime and more leisure for all, and providing appropriate financial incentives and disincentives, the ultimate willingness to adapt to the needs of the microelectronic age must come from employers and employees themselves. They must make, at the level of the local plant and the local community, the adjustments that will be needed if the benefits of the new technologies are to be spread fairly throughout our society.

If the scourge of high unemployment is to be removed from Britain – as it must be, no less on political than on social and moral grounds – we shall need not only faster economic growth and more active labour-market policies, but also new thinking about the relationship between work and leisure. People must be encouraged and helped to stay longer in full-time education and training; to retire earlier; to welcome the opportunity to work fewer hours per week or take longer annual holidays; or to take sabbaticals in the course of their working lives in order to retrain for new careers or simply to engage in private pursuits. We need to look afresh at the role of the volunteer and the voluntary movement, a subject that is discussed in the next chapter, on social responsibilities. In every case, the aim must be to help people see the changing work patterns and greater leisure made possible by the advent of the microelectronic era as a gateway to the achievement of fuller and more satisfying lives.

Intertwined with this objective must be the aim of encouraging people to assume a greater measure of responsibility for insuring against the vicissitudes of life. In Britain reliance on the state has gone too far, and the result has been a loss of drive and dynamism and a playing-down of the importance of market forces as the progenitor of change and progress, casting a shadow over the prospects of future prosperity. More must be done to hand back to the people themselves the responsibility for the decisions which shape their destiny. The *enabling* state should be the objective for the next century; concerned and compassionate about those unable to help themselves, but more selective in choosing its priorities and roles, and more relaxed about the diversities that are part of a free society.

CHAPTER SEVEN

Social Responsibilities

All social primary goods – liberty and opportunity, income and wealth, and the bases of self-respect – are to be distributed equally unless an unequal distribution of any or all of these goods is to the advantage of the least favoured.

John Rawls, *A Theory of Justice*, 1972

Legal rights are different from the rights we call moral, when we have that distinction in mind, because legal rights are rights based in the political history and decisions of the community and have special institutional force against judges in litigation. But legal and 'moral' rights are nevertheless species of a common genus: they are both, in the broader sense I described, creatures of morality.

From a reply by Ronald Dworkin quoted in
M. Cohen, *Contemporary Jurisprudence*, 1984

Britain's post-war social policy programmes – pensions, family allowances and the national health service – led the world. They represented a tide of opinion that was examined, reviewed and copied across the English Channel and admired around the world. Today, alas, the waves usually run in the opposite direction. It is to the continent of Europe rather than the UK that most social reformers who are setting new targets for governments now look. It is in the new world, the United States and Canada, that people search for new ideas from the pioneering work that is being done on inner city decay and urban renewal.

On whatever policy front one wants to choose – education, health, training, social security – other members of the European Community have often achieved what we in Britain are saying is unobtainable or must be postponed. Our membership of the European Community is helping to break the complacent chrysalis within which we have wrapped the reality of our social policies for too long. Teachers, doctors, nurses, welfare-rights workers, have all had their eyes opened by visits to other countries of the Community or by EEC professionals visiting Britain.

One of the myths which has been sown and fostered is the idea that a major reason for Britain's economic decline has been the excessive expenditure on over-lavish social services. The truth is quite the reverse: during the period of economic decline we have had some of the poorest social services in Europe. We are told that we cannot spend more on improving our health, education and social services because this will increase inflation, but our spending has been and is much less than that of other European countries. We no longer have the best welfare state in Europe.

Three stark facts emerge from the various recent studies which have been carried out on European social policies:

• throughout the 1970s social expenditure in the UK grew more slowly than in any of the other eight EEC member states;
• by 1980 the UK was at the bottom of the league, spending barely more than 20 per cent of its GDP on social expenditure compared to the 30 per cent invested by Germany and the Netherlands;
• even the poorest EEC states – Ireland and Italy – were spending proportionately more of their GDP on social expenditure than the UK. The richer states were spending much more.

At whatever point one looks at the education service, we have much to learn from Europe. If one examines the two opposite ends of the service, the under-fives and over-sixteens, one sees the effect of years of low priority being given to education.

Twelve years after Margaret Thatcher, as Secretary of State for Education, first committed herself to achieving within ten years the Plowden Committee's goal of a nursery-school place for 50 per cent of three-year-olds and 90 per cent of four-year-olds, we are nowhere near to achieving this goal. Only 20 per cent of three-year-olds and 40 per cent of four-year-olds at present have places and Mrs Thatcher's education cuts as Prime Minister will reduce these percentages in the next three years. All our European neighbours do better than this. Denmark and Ireland provide places for over 50 per cent of their four-year-olds; Italy, Germany and Luxembourg for over 70 per cent; Belgium and Holland for over 90 per cent and France for all, 100 per cent.

In providing for those over sixteen, even before the present cutbacks, we had the lowest proportion of people aged seventeen to twenty-two in full-time education of any of the ten members of the EEC, with the exception of Ireland. The position has got worse since. Even if we ignore the cuts to the universities, and their senseless emphasis on the technological universities, and look instead at the intermediate level of education – a key area if we are to revitalize our manufacturing industries – we find a disturbing comparison. Is it any wonder that German manufacturing is 50 per cent more productive than British companies, when one compares the training which the workers receive? Germany produces two and a half times as many electricians and twice as many mechanical fitters. The British government's new youth-training scheme will increase the proportion of young people receiving vocational training in the UK but only from 40 per cent of the German level to 60 per cent. Equally serious is the quality of the training. Here again the UK lags behind. One reason for the Germans' high standards is the written and practical tests conducted by outside examiners at the end of their vocational courses – the new UK youth-training scheme shies away from independently set tests.

There is still plenty to be proud of in our NHS in spite of the financial restrictions which the Conservative government has imposed. It is more efficient than most other European systems, and there is a better balance and more cooperation between its separate parts than in many other schemes. But there are grave shortcomings – shortcomings which several European states have been more successful in surmounting. Compared to some European countries we are far less successful in achieving lower mortality figures. There are disturbing inequalities in the distribution of resources – both between regions, between medical specialities and between social classes.

Compared to the professional people in social class one, the unskilled workers of social class five die younger, suffer from more diseases and have fewer of their own teeth; more of the women die in childbirth and the children in infancy. None of these differences are small. Maternal mortality is twice as high, infant mortality four times as high, mortality from bronchitis five times as high and from TB ten times as high in social class five.

One reason why our performance in the health league table is not better has little to do with the NHS – this is the inadequate level of family benefits compared to the benefits paid in some other European states. Child benefits fell by 8 per cent in real terms in the UK between 1979 and 1981, to their lowest level since the frugal 1950s. Other European countries, such as Holland and Germany, cut child benefits too – by 6 and 8 per cent respectively – but in Denmark benefits for a two-child family increased by 40 per cent between 1980 and 1983 and in France by 67 per cent.

The differences between British and European pensions is even more startling. A married couple who retired in 1980 on average earnings received 37 per cent of their net pay in the UK compared to 48 per cent in West Germany, 58 per cent in Holland and 61 per cent in France. The gap for single workers was even wider. Continental Europe has not just been more effective in lifting the level of pensions but has also been more successful in making pension rights transferable for workers changing jobs. France already has universal transferability. Holland plans to follow suit.

The same picture emerges if one looks at unemployment benefit. We hear a lot, in defence of the British government's cuts to social security, about cuts which are being made across Europe. The government, which in five years has made thirteen separate decisions involving social security cuts, implies that they were doing no more than other European states. A recent study has shown how dishonest that assertion is. In Germany, an unemployed worker with two children on average pay has seen his benefit cut from 68 to 63 per cent of net pay. In Holland, on the same basis, the rate has been cut from 85 to 82 per cent. In Britain earnings-related unemployment benefit was abolished altogether. An unemployed worker with two children barely gets more than 50 per cent of net average income. A single worker gets only 25 per cent.

Our European neighbours have demonstrated that high social expenditure does not destroy competitiveness. Our European neighbours, in fact, have shown that investment in social services can actually increase competitiveness – as seen by the results of the German training programmes.

With social inequality widening, it is appropriate to ask how we should create an open, classless and more equal society. How can we eliminate poverty and promote greater equality without stifling enterprise or imposing bureaucracy from the centre? How can we build up the innovating strength of a competitive economy while ensuring a fair distribution of rewards? We need new definitions of social justice and equality which address themselves to the present reality of poverty and deprivation in Britain; we are still dogged by old ideas of social class rooted in the Industrial Revolution.

Social policy which values material equality for its own sake is not the only interpretation of social justice. A better objective would be to maximize the prospects of its worst-off members, very different from the historic objective of the greatest happiness for the greatest number. The onus of proof must be on those who wish to redistribute wealth to show that their proposed course of action will actually improve the position of the worst-off members of society.

A just society can be judged as one in which its worst-off members are as well off as they can be. In such a society the rich might well get richer as long as the prospects of the poor are raised as a consequence and middle incomes are also not jeopardized. Under this definition of equality there is no pretence that all will, or can be equally rewarded, but it deliberately rejects the safety-net society where there is no redistribution above a minimum level of income. The just society does not have to be a crudely levelling society. On the contrary, a social policy would be judged as unjust if its consequences were to reduce the prospects of the worst-off groups. This is not some remote academic point. Some Labour Party policies have in the past substantially damaged Britain's overall economic well-being and its ability to provide for the worst-off groups in society. The poorest groups could be unintentionally damaged by the side-effects of proposed Labour policies – such as a minimum wage, which most research studies show as reducing employment prospects for the less skilled.

A new definition of equality, owing much to the philosophy of John Rawls, would put the focus of policy on the worst-off groups in society. Serious research on poverty and income distribution in Britain has shown that the traditional way in which all political parties look at distributive questions – in terms of wages and salaries, differentials and differences between wages and profits – is extremely unhelpful and is based on obsolete views of class. The worst-off groups are primarily the low paid with dependent children and those who do not work – the elderly, the unemployed, the ethnic minorities, the disabled and single-parent families. It is for this reason that a compassionate and caring society would not always propose the same policies as one aiming at achieving an egalitarian society. An egalitarian society pursued through the traditional class struggle can be neither compassionate nor caring because its motivation is often envious. With the exception of those who are primarily interested in fighting class wars, it is certainly the case that the majority of people in Britain could only be persuaded to support redistributive policies if they felt that the position of the poor was to be demonstrably improved in absolute, not just in relative, terms. They want a combination of policies that creates prosperity and alleviates poverty. This is not unreasonable provided that it is acknowledged that at times of low economic growth, action to help the poorest groups can only be achieved at the expense of those who are better off.

The implications for social policy of starting to think in this way in Britain are profound. A test of whether we should continue with our present policies in the health services, education, housing, pensions and social security would be to ask whether they promote the prospects of the worst-off groups. Another test of whether any social policy is desirable would be to ask whether it is promoting a society with less of a sense of class division – even though adopting such policies would not necessarily mean becoming a more equal society. If it seems more likely that, by giving upper- and middle-income people the same access rights as the poor, the prospects of the latter are diminished rather than increased, then one would question the policy in terms of the principles of social justice, though one might endorse the policy on the grounds of helping to achieve a less class-based society. Much of the universal provision of the post-war welfare state in Britain has achieved less for the poor and more inequality because its coverage has been extended to upper- and middle-income earners. Another problem posed by the conflicting tests of social policy is judging the level at which to set the relatively high marginal rates of taxation on upper and middle-income earners; these taxes are imposed in the name of egalitarianism, but the resultant disincentive effects harm the prospects of the worst-off groups. In policy terms, this is why we must look at possible new taxes on spending and inheritance rather than on earnings and income, and think again about the impact of the present system of taxation on those who invest in production. This means considering what is called an expenditure tax. Tax policy is a complement to both economic and social policy; there is a need to simplify and where possible alter or adjust tax allowances that upset fairness. If the basic objective of social policy is to be improving the lot of the worst-off groups, we need to know in what sense they are worst-off. What is the economic model that describes their prospects and their relationship with better-off groups? The practical problems of such a new approach are clearly enormous because they are so different from the traditional, failed, policy framework.

We need to examine all aspects of social policy from this perspective, starting with social security – transfer payments and benefits – since this is the way in which society can most directly address the problems of the poorest groups and also preserve for them the freedom, inherent in a market economy, to spend their incomes freely. Here, social justice conflicts with the Beveridge principle which implies that everybody who has children, or is sick, or is old, irrespective of personal resources, is entitled to some state benefits. The cost of this has left Britain with a system that is now both inadequate for those who are genuinely in need and, because of the demography of ageing, is likely to be increasingly unaffordable for the taxpayers who have to support it.

The SDP has courageously accepted that these problems can be solved only by a major redistribution of resources through the introduction of a Basic Benefit Scheme aimed at directing state benefits much more accurately, so that they reach the worst-off people, who really need them, and not those who do not. Such a scheme requires a smaller number of different means tests, thus avoiding administrative muddle and cost, but has a much greater impact on poverty. To finance it there has to be an injection of a substantial new sum of money into the social security budget, otherwise there will be no room for manoeuvre to float off all the anomalies of the existing system. One of the least damaging ways of finding this money would be to abolish the married man's tax allowance, which would provide £3.8bn at 1983/4 prices. A much simpler system should be possible when taxes and benefits are integrated; we should then exercise much greater discrimination in deciding who will receive benefits.

The new Basic Benefit would take the place of Family Income Supplement (FIS), rent and rate rebates and free school meals. It would consist of an amount varying according to family size and housing costs. It would go only to those who need it, because it would be gradually withdrawn at a fixed percentage of each extra pound earned, until earnings reach a point at which no more benefit was received.

For those in work and for those receiving an existing national insurance benefit the new Basic Benefit would provide a topping-up of total income. And it would be flexible enough to provide for the needs of people who are neither earning nor receiving a national insurance benefit.

In planning the benefit two main issues arise: first the rate of withdrawal and then the size of the lump-sum amount. Since tax and national insurance already take 39p in the pound, the withdrawal rate must be well below 60p in the pound if we are to avoid the iniquities of the present poverty trap by which people can be worse off after an increase in pay.

But there is a dilemma in choosing the exact withdrawal rate. Let us take the example of a couple with two children earning £80 a week and let us suppose that they qualify for £40 of Basic Benefit. The question now is how rapidly their Basic Benefit should be reduced as they increase their income. A low rate of withdrawal might seem better but it would mean that quite rich families would still be getting Basic Benefit. If, for example, the rate of withdrawal was 20p for every extra pound earned, benefit would still be payable until earnings reached £280 a week. And we should not and cannot afford to subsidize people earning over £14,000 a year. In order to be fair, it would be better to give the extra money to poorer people.

It is tempting to withdraw the Basic Benefit very rapidly as income rises but the objection to this is that the poor would still face very high rates of withdrawal. So one cannot go the whole way down that route either. A middle position would be for families with children, who would receive very substantial help, to have a withdrawal rate of 45p for every extra pound earned and for families without children a withdrawal rate of 25p for every extra pound earned.

Since the Benefit consists of a lump sum minus the amount withdrawn, the next issue is the size of the lump sum, or credit. The credit would have three components: a child credit (which will also take into account the need to compensate for the abolition of the present free school meals), a housing credit (perhaps 60 per cent of rent and rates and an equivalent amount for mortgage relief), plus a personal credit (with different rates to take account of the different needs of single people and couples). The personal credit would also take into account the need to compensate for the abolition of FIS.

A single person would be eligible for the single personal credit and the housing credit; a family of four, say, would be eligible for the personal credit for a couple, credits for the two children and the housing credit. For example, at 1983/4 prices, a couple earning £80 a week, paying £21 per week in rent and rates and with two children, one of whom is under five, would be eligible for a credit of £51 per week. This is calculated as follows:

Personal credit for a couple	£31.00
Credit for the first child	£46.00
Credit for the second child	£ 3.20
Housing credit (60 per cent of £21)	£12.60
	£92.80

But since 45p of benefit is withdrawn for every pound earned, £36 must be deducted (i.e. 45 per cent of £80)	−£41.76
leaving a credit of	£51.04

One of the main aims would be to concentrate help on families with children. That is why the child credit in the Basic Benefit would be generous, with special help for the first child, and the existing Child Benefit would continue to be paid on top of the proposed benefits.

Basic Benefit would help people trapped in their poverty because, under the present rules, they incur lower benefits and higher taxes as their incomes rise; they are ensnared and cannot prosper. Small wonder that the black economy has grown so fast. The key fact is that the present government has increased the lowest marginal rate of income tax plus national insurance contributions from 31 per cent in 1979 to 39 per cent in 1983. The taxation of low-income families has been growing steadily over the last thirty years. In 1950 the tax threshold for a married man with two children was about two thirds of average earnings, well above the defined poverty line. In 1983 people started to pay tax when they earned only a third of average earnings, well below the current poverty line, which has risen with better standards of living. Simplifying and reforming the tax system cannot just stop with the introduction of Basic Benefit. We must take a careful look at redressing the balance of taxation between earners and owners and especially the owners who spend heavily out of capital but do not invest. Capital taxes bring in barely a billion pounds a year, equal to roughly 1p on income tax and less than half as much as was raised by capital gains tax and estate duty a decade ago. That goes some way towards explaining why the tax system has not done more to reduce inequalities. If we link the proposed Basic Benefit with serious tax reform, we will grapple with the very real problem of low pay; we will create, in effect, a minimum wage, and achieve far more than would ever come from minimum-wage legislation.

The state pension scheme is oddly a social security payment that gives more to those who have earned more – an expensive decision justified at the time by the inadequacy of the private pension system. But if private schemes are made portable as of right, structural changes in the state pension scheme would then be worth considering. A truly radical reform of pensions would be to leave more resources to be targeted more selectively at the central problem: poverty in old age. If the prime interest of reform is to reduce overall social security expenditure, rather than target more expenditure more effectively to the task of abolishing poverty, then it will never attract the consensus across different governments that is so vital.

If one looks at the NHS from the standpoint of social justice, one can argue that it is probably unjust that a person on well above average earnings in Britain should enjoy free health services, because in service terms the universal provision can be said to harm the prospects of the worst-off groups. Those who could make adequate provision for themselves through private health insurance would in theory release extra resources to assist the prospects of the worst-off. But there are serious grounds for opposing such a two-nation health service. In reality this would do away with the concept of need – not ability to pay – as being the best allocator of scarce health resources. Rightly, there are grounds other than egalitarianism for rejecting an extension of the marketplace into a health-care system, where demand will always be infinite. It would also damage the chances of achieving a more open, classless society.

Much the same arguments lead one to conclude that an extension of the marketplace in education should be rejected. Indeed, allowing private education to spread would have much more profound consequences for perpetuating class division than would probably come from the present increase in private health provision.

It is in housing that we see some of the worst consequences of social policy, in terms of class segregation and limitation of opportunities, for the least well off. The whole system has worked to reduce choice and to create greater barriers between communities. Inner city areas have built a great deal of council housing and done far too little to give housing opportunities to middle-income groups at the same time. They have thus created forms of segregation which have led to unbalanced communities and reduced opportunities in employment and education. In the suburbs of the cities, by contrast, there has been little building of low-cost rented housing. There could be a variety of providers for rented housing, with building societies and pension funds investing in low-cost rented housing, as well as local government. People need to be given a chance to form neighbourhood trusts to take over their own estates and there needs to be a concentration of public funds on raising standards in the worst estates. Advocating a Tenants' Charter has little meaning when it establishes rights which are not matched by financial resources.

Another area of social policy where there is a failure to match rights and resources relates to the ethnic minorities. Racial justice and racial harmony will only be achieved if it is the objective of as wide a cross-section as possible of our society. All political parties need to go out of their way to demonstrate publicly their concern about the growth of racial prejudice. In local elections the National Front has polled as high as 15–19 per cent in some wards. We cannot pretend that the National Front does not exist, and we will not reduce its influence by trying to ignore it. We must defeat their prejudices by tackling the social discontent on which their prejudices breed.

It is natural of course that the particular interests and problems of the ethnic communities will require them to seek redress through their own community groups and welfare organizations. It would be extremely dangerous, however, and socially divisive and de-stabilizing if this should be the exclusive channel for the political activities of non-white Britons. The black community, whether they be of Asian or of Afro-Caribbean origin, must play a full and active part in our national political parties; that participation should be reflected in party office holders and party candidates at both local and parliamentary level. That is by far the best way of confronting and confounding the National Front in areas where their appeal is increasing. Any concept of separate development for ethnic minorities, either in terms of establishing their own political groupings or in having separate status within existing political parties, should be firmly rejected as being unacceptable and essentially repugnant to those who want to see a multi-racial society as a working reality. It would perpetuate the very problems and divisions which it sought superficially to solve and postpone the attaining of a society which is free from racial prejudice or discrimination.

To achieve that end will require hard work and effort, and not simply tokenism, by all political parties. It will require an under-standing of each other's problems and a shared appreciation of problems common to all. One does not need to be black or brown or yellow to be inadequately housed, or to be worried about the safety of our streets, the education of our children, the general standards of health care or the prospects of finding a job. These are common problems, the solution of which can best be achieved by concerted action.

New thinking is urgently needed on the subject of immigration. While the Conservative government is presiding over an unprecedented shifting of power from the courts to officials acting in the name of the Home Secretary, all Labour does is bleat about generalities and promise to repeal existing legislation.

Yet immigration legislation in some form or other is here to stay – as a result of Britain's history and, even more fundamentally, because of the economic inequality between north and south, it is an unavoidable fact that more people will wish to come here than can reasonably be admitted.

The government, on the other hand, are constantly justifying what appear to be harsh decisions on individuals on the grounds that a policy which is 'firm and fair' will always have to seem more firm than fair in individual cases. A restrictive policy need not be harsh on individuals provided that the Home Secretary shows flexibility and understanding.

Wherever possible administrative discretion should be exercised on objective grounds and subject to effective judicial review. The concentration of discretionary power in the hands of officials makes it possible for rights which exist under the law to be virtually nullified by administrative delay. A wife of a man lawfully settled here has the right to join her husband but she needs an entry certificate. Women applying for entry certificates in Bangladesh – attempting to exercise their statutory rights – are in 1984 told to return to the British High Commission for interview in 1986.

Some of the arbitrary powers provided to the Home Office in the 1971 Immigration Act are being looked at by the courts and some recent judgements in the High Court may be the beginning of a slow process by which the balance is being redressed. But it remains true, for example, that a suspected illegal entrant – someone who has gained entry by deception, for example by falsely pretending to be the close dependant of a person already settled here – may be removed without a deportation order and with no right of appeal. Given the present climate it is inevitable that some people are being removed who may have a claim to remain, possibly because the illegality may have been unwitting. Some are of good character, some have married here and have British wives and children.

Where such a person maintains his or her innocence there

should clearly be a right of appeal. In other cases, too, the ethnic minorities have good cause for complaint about the rules, and their operation, which harshly affect them.

Under the Immigration Rules introduced in 1983, following the failure of the government to secure approval of the first set because of an odd parliamentary alliance of the opposition and the Conservative right, an entry certificate is to be refused to a man wishing to join a British woman here for marriage if the 'primary purpose' of the marriage is, in the opinion of the entry certificate officer, to obtain entry to the UK. British girls of Asian origin are finding it extremely difficult to bring in husbands under the arranged marriage system because of the operation of this rule. There is in any case a requirement that the parties to the proposed marriage should have met.

Under the new rules it is virtually impossible for a settled immigrant to bring in his/her elderly parents for settlement. This particularly affects the Asians; every week old men and women from the Indian subcontinent are turned back at airports on the grounds that although they claim that they are coming for a visit they will really stay for settlement, for which the conditions are extremely stringent. The handling of this issue could easily be made more humanitarian. Though the problem is now largely 'solved', those UK-citizen Asians who went to India when the emergency blew up in Kenya are having to wait inordinately long in India for a visa to come here. The delay is about seven years; it seems entirely unnecessary, given that the numbers are not large, to maintain an arbitrary quota of 500 vouchers a year for Asians in India who are British citizens.

Basically, less inscrutability is needed and much more scope for judicial review. The way the control is operated needs to be changed, particularly the right of appeal and the delays which characterize both the immigration-control system and the appeals process.

The care of children is an area of social policy particularly involving rights and responsibilities. We should review carefully the 1975 Children Act. What has the Act achieved? It has first and foremost placed children's interests in the centre of the stage. It has helped change attitudes and forced us to recognize that children have interests as well as their parents. Some people believe we have gone too far, but this is to forget the way in which children's rights were being disregarded prior to the Act. The Act helped make adoption an acceptable alternative for children in care – particularly older children in care. Almost 25 per cent of children adopted in 1981 were over five, compared to less than 10 per cent in 1970, excluding step-parent adoptions. It has given foster-parents more rights should they want to adopt, for after five years of caring those foster-parents who make an adoption application cannot have the child taken away before the court hearing. It has also given adopted people the right of access to their birth records, which has proceeded reasonably smoothly.

There has been much more involvement of parents and foster-parents in decisions – such as stopping access – than before. A new right introduced only in 1984 allows parents to appeal to the courts if access is stopped. There has been an increasing emphasis on seeking the opinion of the child – previously no one under eleven was ever asked for their opinion and those over eleven only occasionally. There has been much more involvement of councillors and courts – making social workers more accountable. Social workers did have too much unfettered power in the past, a danger for any profession. Now, in certain areas, like access, there is an appeal to the courts, and in other areas, like the assumption of parental rights, social workers' decisions must be reviewed by councillors. The inarticulate now have more avenues of appeal, and many more decisions have to be recorded and written down.

All this, of course, has to be set against other developments; the squeeze on social services, particularly in the local-authority areas most in need of help; the successive cuts to social security, which has put families in poverty under even more pressure; the lack of any coherent family policy by successive governments; the government's plans – as revealed in the leak of the family-policy group's papers – to exploit the family, particularly married women, to pick up the burden of the welfare state.

We need a much more coherent approach to family policy, embracing local and central government and voluntary bodies. An annual report on the family, as the Standing Commission on the Family recommended, needs to be accompanied by a family-impact statement on all government decisions affecting the family.

Children need to be given more priority across the board, from social security to the High Court. No European state has been particularly outstanding in its support for children, but the UK has been behind much of Europe.

We need to face up to the biggest social change in post-war Britain: the arrival of mass divorce. Three decades ago only one out of ten marriages ended in divorce. Today, one out of three couples who marry can expect their marriage to break up. We need a nationwide conciliation service for separating couples, to reduce custody and access fights, and we need a family court, where the bench can specialize and become familiar with the problems. To date this government has inexplicably refused to go ahead with either. It has turned down the idea of subsidies for conciliation and almost killed the only full-time service in the country, in Bristol. It has retreated from its earlier hopes of a family court, because certain vested interests in the law thought it might threaten their income or status.

Looking to the future of fostering, it is right to want a review of current practice, for the Houghton Committee concentrated on adoption, as did the 1975 Children Act, and it is right to insist on children being given more priority by social services departments and to push for more training for social workers. Only sixty-two local authorities are paying the suggested minimum allowance for fostering under-fives and even fewer for sixteen- to seventeen-year-olds. But if central government legislates, that raises difficult issues of principle in relation to the necessary autonomy of local authorities. Written agreements for each foster-home placement, easier procedures for parents to challenge decisions and more specialization by social workers are desirable.

We need to look in greater depth at the effects of long-term fostering. Would adoption be a better solution? What is the breakdown rate? Will we always need short-term fostering and adolescent fostering. We need to develop contract fostering, as pioneered by Lambeth, so that all parties know what is required of them, and give all the encouragement we can to the goal of improving the status and skills of foster parents.

Social welfare policies should aim primarily to do two things. First, they should make generous provision for the individuals who, for one reason or another, cannot fend well for themselves in our increasingly competitive societies. Secondly, they should aim to break down the discrimination and inequalities of power which often accompany and increase material deprivation, enabling all to feel that they can make a useful contribution to the community in which they live. It is becoming ever clearer that only a partnership between formal and informal policies and practices can hope to achieve such objectives.

Policies to assist the least well off should give a much greater emphasis to cash assistance, which they can allocate themselves. This redistributes power as well as income. It is simpler, it provides a greater element of choice for many and avoids the problems, with which we are all too familiar, of those on relatively high incomes being better at 'working the system' of the welfare state and getting more out of it than do lower-income groups. None the less, redistribution of cash can clearly not meet all the potential needs. Many of the things that the voluntary and statutory services provide are on a communal basis. They could not be, nor should they be, bought in the market by individuals. There is also a limit to the amount of income redistribution which is either politically feasible or socially just. Philosophers like John Rawls are correct to stress that it is wrong to impose redistributive taxation in such a way that the poorest members of society actually became worse off rather than better off – due to a poorly performing economy – or to stimulate the emergence of a 'black economy' outside the scope of the tax system, thus generating only scant benefits for the poor. The importance of Rawls's writings on equality is that they establish the moral and theoretical framework for a theory of social rights, for the welfare state, in terms which are neither paternalist nor statist.

The closer one comes to the entirely state-provided end of the spectrum of welfare provision, the more difficult it becomes to incorporate measures which retain the power of the citizen. Inevitably, any locally or centrally controlled government social administration has to have rules. As we have moved towards establishing more rights for the citizen in social welfare so we have inevitably moved away from discretion and flexibility. As we publish criteria and rules, so we limit the scope for discretion. Social security benefits and local government housing benefits have an inbuilt rigidity, as being 'fair' between applicants dominates. Increasingly the interpretation of criteria and rules has become bureaucratized. As more people become eligible for selective assistance, so the machinery of administration becomes more automatic and impersonal. Other professionals may well act as advocates, aiming to ensure that clients do as well as they can 'within the rules'; but the overall structure of the rules is not open to negotiation or modification for the individual, except in the democratic process through councils and Parliament.

The entirely informal, mainly voluntary, caring networks often provide almost exactly the reverse of the characteristics of the formal systems of state welfare provision. The characteristics of informal care networks are flexibility, their focus is on particular, often narrowly defined, citizen groups and often, especially in the newer self-help groups, there are no inequalities of power or imbalance between 'carer' and 'cared for'. But at the same time, provision for particular groups in need varies widely both between regions and between groups. There are undoubtedly some groups or individuals which are not served at all. Neither does the distribution of voluntary effort between sectors reflect the optimum deployment of resources to meet social need.

The danger of extolling the merits and strengths of the voluntary sector is that it can easily be portrayed as a cutting back on professional and statutory provision, or a way of penny pinching. Far too often, governments have talked about community care while acting to inhibit care within the community. The trained professional social worker is an indispensable part of our personal social services. But we need to rethink the central tasks that should be the responsibility of the valued and expensively trained professional. While the trained professionals aim always to retain certain direct responsibilities for a number of individuals, far more emphasis needs to be placed on the strategic responsibilities of the professional; on matters such as ready access to services, accountability and, particularly, on supervising volunteers, and galvanizing the latent resources within neighbourhoods in Britain.

It has been estimated that there are over 14,000 paid staff in the voluntary sector in the UK and this is probably an underestimate. Sixteen million hours are estimated as being worked by volunteers each week in the statutory and voluntary sectors and there are some one and a quarter million 'carers', mostly women, who take prime responsibility for a handicapped or sick person.

Volunteers, therefore, in both the statutory and the voluntary sectors are central. Each week volunteers are providing the equivalent in hours of 400,000 full-time social workers – excluding the informal home-based 'carers'. Though 'productivity' of volunteers may often be lower than that of social workers, and they are often doing very different jobs, the key role of the volunteers is clear.

In our society many feel that they wish to contribute voluntary help but have no outlet for their energies or concerns, although there is much work to be done. Elderly people living alone find it impossible to maintain their garden, to paint their walls. There is no one to do their shopping, no one to insulate their ceilings or attics or weatherproof their windows, and all too many of our elderly suffer from hypothermia. It is an indictment of the way we organize our society that so many of our inner cities should look like wastelands, despite the fact that many people, given the chance, could and would contribute to improving that environment – which is all too often their own. It is folly to allow the amenities which could create leisure opportunities for millions, such as rivers and canals, to be filled with rubbish or to become overgrown with weeds. It is mindless insensitivity to incarcerate in institutions people who could live happy lives in the community outside if only they could have a little basic support.

We need to organize society so that we can make better use of voluntary effort. This enabling is not about finding resources to maintain the level of services we have got now, but about how we can release additional resources to build a far better society, in which hope, dignity and a full life are available to all our citizens, where there is a transformation of the entire pattern of social relations from exploitation to mutual aid. There is an appalling mismatch of resources in our society to which a man from Mars would surely point with amazement within hours of landing – intolerable unemployment levels, intolerable deterioration in social provision. The Conservative government does nothing about this mismatch because they are locked in hostility to all forms of increased public expenditure. The Labour Party does nothing because they are tied to supporting public service unions and committed to sustaining universal state provision, and so cannot break loose to think of new ways of dealing with this mismatch.

Today we need to ask ourselves why, with so many tasks unfulfilled and needs unmatched, does our society not organize a new imaginative Voluntary Community Service Scheme so that all of its citizens can contribute to the community and none live in enforced idleness? A slight mismatch is a price we all accept for an unregimented society. A large mismatch might have been temporarily acceptable for a few years, but is it really tolerable that we should continue the current gross mismatch of resources, which has gone on for at least eight years, and is certainly likely to be with us whatever the government for many more years to come? Are we prepared to go on seeing the young, the active middle-aged and the elderly people who want to contribute to alleviating hardship and social distress in society condemned not just to idleness but to feeling rejected, being unable to contribute to society?

We are at last beginning to arrange for better training and job experience for the school leavers aged sixteen to eighteen, though there is still much to do. Yet today when many of them have already gone through such schemes, 380,000 eighteen- to twenty-year-olds are still left without any activity to contribute to society, with no tasks to fulfil, let alone a proper job. We are becoming a rootless and fragmented society, a society where the objective is to clamber into the lifeboat but then, once aboard, to be unconcerned about those who are still adrift. We are in danger of losing a whole generation of people, who will be turned off from the society in which they live because they have been deprived of the opportunity to contribute to it. Too many of them have been given neither rights nor responsibilities.

In typical British fashion, up to now successive governments have tinkered with the problem rather than attempting a fundamental reassessment. We have reached this situation because of repeated mistaken post-war assumptions. Aneurin Bevan's view that once the National Health Service was operating effectively the health of the nation would so improve that the percentage of GNP that we would need to devote to health could drop was holy writ well into the 1950s. The consensus view all through the 1970s, with politicians responding to need and to the advice of experts, was that there was no alternative but to go on continuously expanding public provision and investing in professionals. Wiser now, more and more people recognize that the demands of health care are infinite, that the demands of community care with an ever ageing population, with people living on with serious handicaps, can never be met solely by increasing professionally trained staff. We have to involve more people in community concerns, ensure that the consumer voice is heard and that services respond more closely to what people want. More expenditure is vital but money is not the only resource. To admit this is not to endorse a political approach that is afraid of trying to persuade the electorate to finance higher levels of social expenditure – it is to recognize that we cannot begin to meet all the pressing social needs by increasing taxes and hiring others to do our caring for us. We need more professionals, but we need to concentrate their skills. We need to build a partnership between the formal and informal or the professional and the lay which will provide for a major expansion in 'informal' care while making sure that strategic planning provides for the needs of certain groups and that major inequalities between different deprived groups are prevented. That means spending money, of course, but it means spending it in different, new ways.

The sums involved in voluntary sector spending are small compared with the numbers of people involved. The Voluntary Services Unit of the Home Office estimated total central government departmental expenditure on voluntary organizations in 1982/3 at around £151m. Manpower Services Commission (MSC) voluntary sector programmes in the year to the end of 1983 amounted to a further £139m. Total expenditure on supporting 280 volunteer bureaux has been estimated at under £10m. Voluntary care is not care on the cheap but it is a fact that the costs of a really significant expansion of the resources available to the voluntary sector would be low.

A Voluntary Community Service Scheme would need to be very different from the four schemes currently existing to encourage volunteering but which are designed only for the unemployed and lie outside the purely skilled training provision.

The Community Programme which is run by the Manpower Services· Commission currently provides around 130,000 temporary employment opportunities for long-term unemployed people on local community projects. Participants are paid an average of £60 per week although employers are asked to top this up to equal the hourly rate for the job. Another scheme is the Voluntary Projects Programme introduced in August 1982 and administered by the MSC. It aims to create a variety of opportunities for unemployed people to enable them to do voluntary work without affecting their entitlement to statutory benefits. This scheme currently provides about 25,000 voluntary opportunities for unemployed people and costs £8m.

Opportunities for Volunteering is a smaller project costing £4m; it is run by the DHSS along the same lines as the Voluntary Projects Programme. There is also, in a rather different category, the Armed Services Youth Training Scheme, run by the Ministry of Defence, which aims to provide one-year cadetships for sixteen-year-olds in the armed services. In the first year 2,000 places were available on this scheme and over 3,000 serious applications were received. However, due to the stiff entry requirements laid down, only 600 of these applications were taken up.

The problem with these schemes are that they mix the concept of community service with the essential task of skill training. Skill training should stand on its own as the highest priority; it is not to be confused in any way with the suggested Volunteer Community Service Scheme. The current Youth Training Scheme should as soon as possible be expanded to two years and its training element should be considerably increased. We should also try to find money to provide education maintenance allowances, to remove the incentive to leave school at the age of sixteen to bring in money either from a job or from unemployment benefit. These are very expensive new expenditure commitments and reinforce the case for thinking afresh about how to find less expensive ways of meeting society's many other needs.

If we are going to attempt to increase substantially the number of people volunteering their services to others, we cannot do so only by reinforcing what already exists, although that is the essential first step. The role of the state is primarily an enabling one, to make the most of voluntary resources. It does not make sense to impose vast programmes without experimentation first to see what works and what does not. A depressing testament to the centralizing and bureaucratizing tendencies of governments in the UK is the wreckage of previous universal-panacea schemes for increasing the use of volunteers. No one proposal will have all the answers; the aim must be to foster diversity, and to give projects the resources to go their own ways. At the same time there does exist in our country a tremendous amount of goodwill which is not yet being tapped by the voluntary sector – partly because the institutions to use it do not exist, partly because of lack of money. This is especially the case with the use of full-time volunteers.

A major problem for such projects is to find the money to pay the volunteers their living expenses plus a few pounds extra a week. The first thing that the government must do if it wants to encourage a Volunteer Community Service Scheme-using full-time volunteers is to make available to public or charitable bodies which can make good use of it money for paying volunteers.

We can learn a lot from the examples of other countries. Groups such as the California Conservation Corps make use of full-time residential volunteers in an enormous and demanding range of projects, from environmental improvement to fighting forest fires. The West German Zivildienst uses 36,000 conscientious objectors each year – largely with the elderly and housebound, in the 'Mobile Social Help' scheme. Several common factors stand out from all these schemes, and from the strong response in the UK to such schemes as the adult-literacy programme, where 50,000 people volunteered as tutors on a one-to-one basis.

There is a need to capture the imaginations of those who are willing to become involved in their local community life. Full-time volunteering has a bad name in the UK because of its associations with lack of success in the labour market, and with make-work schemes of a depressing and uninspiring nature. If a scheme is going to succeed, it has to be imaginative – attracting both the most academically able and the least, the most practically talented and the most cack-handed.

If a Volunteer Community Service Scheme is seen primarily as a scheme to occupy idle hands, then it will never have the appeal and the worth of a scheme that is seen as being designed to help meet society's needs. We need to harness the spirit and motivation that lay behind the founding of the Peace Corps and Voluntary

Service Overseas to contribute to our own society here at home. It is not necessary to go to Botswana to see poverty and deprivation, you can see them in Wandsworth, in Notting Hill, in Brixton and Toxteth. Rightly, volunteer programmes in the developing world – where there are insufficient professionally trained people to supervise the unskilled volunteers – have increasingly tended to rely on the mature and the more skilled volunteers. But here in Britain we have a substantial body of professionally trained staff capable of providing the supervising infrastructure; so the same constraints do not apply.

In helping to meet those needs, a properly designed Volunteer Community Service Scheme would, as an important secondary feature, provide those who have no job but who wish to contribute to society with a fulfilling and useful task. Its primary function, however, would be seen as part of a national voluntary effort to correct some of society's deficiencies and to carry out tasks that will not be done under any plans conceivable at present for expansion of the numbers of the professionally trained.

A Voluntary Community Service Scheme must have wide appeal, with young and old contributing, whether they have good job prospects or not. It is essential to attract into such a scheme people who have good job prospects – young people who are due to go on to university, polytechnic or college, and those in work who might wish to take early retirement or take a sabbatical year to contribute.

At present Community Service Volunteers (CSV) places volunteers from all ability ranges, university entrants and borstal boys. It is explicitly committed to placing everyone who applies. But CSV is now fully booked for places and waiting lists for their projects are long. For a new Volunteer Community Service Scheme to succeed on a scale that matches the need there must be developed an ethos in society that welcomes the spirit of service, wants to encourage it, sees merit in those who contribute to it. Employers and universities would hopefully recognize the improvement in maturity and responsibility that undertaking community service gives to applicants for jobs and places. Eventually one might need to establish the right of people to be released to volunteer.

There are many who would welcome enhanced opportunities

to contribute to the community for around a year between school and higher education and perhaps reinforce this with a further few weeks' contribution every year for a period. A future nurse or doctor might choose to serve in a mentally handicapped hospital or hostel, a future engineer on an environmental project. Someone going into industry might like to volunteer for the armed forces for a year only, but then continue with a heavy training commitment as a reserve. An accounts clerk might well wish to administer a community project for a one- or two-year period. Everyone would maintain their benefit entitlement and have out-of-pocket expenses. In appropriate cases there would need to be some additional supplement. Institutional barriers which now sometimes force potential volunteers to choose between service and their future career chances must be swept away and positive incentives given to volunteer (but not negative incentives, which would risk identifying the whole scheme with compulsion).

Amongst the critics of such a Volunteer Community Service Scheme are, from past experience, professionals who will see it as undermining standards, even though there is no intention of diluting their professionalism. Some unions will see it as reducing job opportunities and their membership numbers, but that is alarmist and is not the intention. Some politicians will not wish to incur this type of added expenditure – most Conservatives, because they prefer no increase in public expenditure, most people in the Labour Party because they are geared to advocating increasing existing conventional expenditure patterns. These are arguments for the status quo. Only those sufficiently free of vested interest will wish first to investigate a Volunteer Community Service Scheme and, if it stands serious scrutiny, champion it and develop the vital public consensus for its success.

The tasks for the volunteers need to be ones where their being volunteers will be an asset. In an old people's home, where staff are often too busy to spend much time talking to individual residents, volunteers can provide a stimulus, organize play readings and help with personal projects – tasks which can dramatically affect the quality of life for people in the home and where the volunteers' freshness and enthusiasm outweigh their inexperience. The same is true of a whole host of tasks in other institutions. It is true of much back-breaking work in the fields of conservation and environmental improvement, work that would not be undertaken if it had to be paid for in the market. The enterprising work-camps run by the National Trust are an example.

The importance of giving real areas of responsibility to volunteers is increasingly being recognized and this means giving them some power to determine how their tasks should be performed and what those tasks should be. It means giving them influence in the national and local management of the scheme and allocation of funds. This is essential, both from the point of view of motivation and because the experience of volunteering should in itself improve the ability of volunteers to take more control over their own lives.

The training of the volunteer is crucial, for whereas small numbers of full-time volunteers can probably learn on the job, large numbers might well be more trouble than they are worth unless they have some idea of what to do and how to help before they arrive on a project. Both the California Corps and the Zivildienst have training periods of from three weeks to a month and it is becoming recognized that this is the essential prerequisite for success.

On the whole people do not want to help something as abstract as 'society'. They want to help the environment, or old people, or children, or the handicapped. Schemes to foster more full-time volunteering must be geared to individuals and to localities. The present Voluntary Services Unit in the Home Office does not have the ministerial or political weight behind it to raise public consciousness of the opportunities to contribute. It would help to have a senior minister committed to introducing and promoting a Volunteer Community Service Scheme, but there is much to be said for 'franchising' the management of any scheme to national or local bodies active in particular fields.

Project aid, as distinct from financial support for individuals, would have to start small – aiding either particular geographical areas, or particular sectors, or experimental schemes. As with CSV now, or the California Conservation Corps, or the proposal of the Mayor of New York, Ed Koch, for a similar scheme, there is likely to be much more demand for places on the scheme than there are places available, at least to start with. It would be important, as is proposed in New York, to choose the volunteers in a way which preserved the social mix of the applicants; the scheme must not become a magnet for high fliers or a ghetto for the unemployed.

Simply because of the logistics of time, volunteering would attract more young people than middle-aged people – it can be easier to take six months or a year off at the age of eighteen than at the age of thirty-five, especially if one is paid only one's living expenses and a little more. This is not a bad thing, as long as we do not forget the value of involving those with experience, the contribution which can come from those who are retired. Eventually most young people might be involved in one form of community service or another, where possible full time. If we truly want to make our society fairer and more compassionate, giving people the chance to become involved in social problems early in their lives is a good way to start. But it would be disappointing if such a scheme were only to attract young people – it would build up its numbers more quickly if there were a significant involvement of the retired and of people on secondment from other jobs – those who are often best equipped to help professionals with their supervision.

There are some obvious pitfalls for a Volunteer Community Service Scheme. It must contain no hint of compulsion, and must not go too fast too soon, yet it must be sufficiently ambitious from the start to capture the imagination of the public. It must build on and not disrupt existing partnerships between formal and informal patterns of care. It must not spawn new bureaucracies. The scheme must not be aimed at curbing unemployment – it must be seen as a permanent mechanism for enriching society, not as a shabby makeshift by a society which fails to provide paid work for many of its people. Above all, the scheme must not become a substitute for good, thorough, job-related training for all. That is one reason why it should not cover those under eighteen. The Tawney Society in their pamphlet *Count Us In* (obtainable at 18 Victoria Park Square, London E2 9PF) estimates costs in different ways; 100,000 places could be created at an estimated gross cost of £230m and a net cost of £104m. Half a million places could be created at an estimated net cost of under £500m or a gross cost of £1.2bn.

The opportunities far outweigh all the obvious obstacles; we have to move with vigour and enthusiasm to give those who might wish to contribute to society as full-time volunteers the means to do so. There is very considerable support amongst the public for an expansion of full-time volunteering and increased opportunities for investment in community affairs. Well over 50 per cent of young people are in favour of the idea, indicating that a Volunteer Community Service Scheme is an overdue national initiative that could have a profound social impact.

Increasing all forms of informal care should be a major goal of government – both because it will enable us to get to grips with many social problems that now seem insoluble and because of its ability to play a major part in changing the nature of our society and the ways in which people relate to one another.

Increased automation and productivity give the chance of creating a society where men and women are not shut in organizational boxes all their lives, but can play a diverse and changing part in the activities of their community. Phased retirement, the shorter working week and more people working from offices at home all provide opportunities for greater flexibility. It is no longer enough to think that we can divide our lives, slough off our responsibilities, pay others to do our caring for us. A whole and a healthy society demands that each of us plays a part, so that formal and informal networks of social provision can strengthen and support one another, and so that power can be effectively shared between the state and its citizens.

Britain cannot meet its social responsibilities to all its citizens, given the extent of current deprivation and poverty, without the political courage to advocate a fairer distribution of resources. Aiming for the maximum justice in society, as described by John Rawls, and for a society of equal concern and respect for equal rights, as described by Ronald Dworkin, is likely to prove more inspiring than advocating equality of income, a goal in which few believe and even fewer are prepared to work for.

CHAPTER EIGHT

Caring for
the Whole Person

Tender-minded and tough-minded people, characterized as I have written them down, do both exist. Each of you probably knows some well-marked example of each type, and you know what each example thinks of the example on the other side of the line. They have a low opinion of each other. Their antagonism, whenever as individuals their temperaments have been intense, has formed in all ages a part of the philosophic atmosphere of the time. It forms a part of the philosophic atmosphere today. The tough think of the tender as sentimentalists and soft-heads. The tender feel the tough to be unrefined, callous, or brutal.

William James, *Pragmatism*, 1907

The National Health Service is not safe with this government; the reasons for this are both philosophical and financial. The philosophical reason is grounded in the ideological stance of Thatcherism, an approach that wants the marketplace and market values not just in commercial policy but in social policy as well; an approach that sees a market in health care and in education; that fails to understand that toughness and tenderness can go together.

The symbol of Thatcherism must be what the Prime Minister does, not just what she says. It is no intrusion into Mrs Thatcher's private life to ask why, if she wishes the country to believe her government is supportive of the NHS, she does not use its facilities herself when she needs medical attention. We would, given her views, expect her to be covered by private insurance, but as Prime Minister she cannot in this, as in other matters, be judged only as a private citizen.

She is, like every citizen, free to buy private medicine if that is what she wants. But she is the ultimate employer of over a million people who work for the NHS. When she uses a private day clinic for a varicose vein operation one can excuse it, even while not endorsing it, on the grounds that she at least did not add to the existing waiting-list for non-urgent surgery. (A side benefit was that it demonstrated publicly that there is no reason for the NHS continuing as a routine practice to make varicose veins an in-patient operating procedure. Many surgical practices which doctors use to increase throughput in private hospitals should also be more widely used by those same doctors when operating in the NHS.)

But the Prime Minister went on to flaunt her use of private-sector medicine in front of the whole world by having the serious operation on her retina also in a private clinic. Such acute eye surgery has no waiting-list in the NHS and the quality of treatment is of the highest international standard. What a boost for morale within the NHS and for its standing, if Mrs Thatcher had seen fit to use an NHS hospital and been seen publicly thanking NHS surgeons, nurses and staff after a successful outcome. The country rightly senses a deep-seated repudiation by the Prime Minister of the philosophical basis of the NHS, and scant regard for the justice of a health-care system organized on the basis of need rather than the ability to pay.

The financial reason why the NHS is not safe with the government is that they are not spending enough to cover essential needs. Few of us are aware of how little, comparatively, we in Britain spend on health care. In the United States and West Germany the total health spending, both private and public, amounts to 10 per cent of GNP. In Britain it is only about 6 per cent, but the NHS has given Britain a more cost-effective service. It has been possible to tolerate existing levels of spending because the NHS has more family-concentrated and community-based patterns of service than is possible under a fee-for-service insurance scheme.

The standard of care for people with very serious illnesses or who have had serious accidents is on average far better in Britain than in the United States. A lower proportion of our elderly citizens are in institutional care than in continental Europe or America, because we have a superior system for achieving health care and more support in the home. Our district nursing and health-visiting services are virtually unique to Britain and give invaluable help to families at very low cost. Our family-doctor service flourishes, in spite of problems with deputizing services in some areas, and yet this service has virtually disappeared in most other countries. The Royal Commission on the NHS said in 1979: 'the NHS is not suffering from a mortal disease susceptible to heroic surgery. Already the NHS has achieved a great deal and embodies aspirations and ideals of great value.'

The Commission endorsed the view that to improve performance was a hard-slogging job. Even the Treasury has accepted that the NHS requires a minimal inflation-proof growth in expenditure of 1–1.5 per cent merely to maintain existing standards. The serious charge against the government is that they are cutting expenditure well below this critical level and cutting funds to the rest of the NHS in order to pay inescapable extra costs such as the GPs' increased drug bill.

During its first four years this government did provide this essential expenditure growth and from 1979 to 1982 NHS staff numbers increased by 2.3 per cent, as opposed to an increase of only 1.4 per cent from 1976 to 1979. The cuts to manpower imposed after the 1983 General Election meant, however, that in 1984, for the first time since 1948, the service had fewer people at the end of the financial year than at the start.

There have been some local reductions, not redeployment, of nurses and physiotherapists, as well as managers, porters and other ancillary staff. These staff cuts have been precipitate, confusing and extremely damaging to future development. They were arbitrarily imposed from the centre in the middle of the financial year. Staffing changes sometimes become necessary, of course, with different patterns of health care, but if the standards of service are to improve, the NHS should be redirecting staff effort into community, geriatric and psychiatric care, and particularly preventative action on health. It is a sad commentary that, between 1950 and 1980, funding of hospital-based services rose by 7.8 per cent while spending on community and GP services fell by 1.6 per cent and 3.9 per cent respectively.

The number of people over seventy-five will increase by 60 per cent in the next two decades. The reason why this statistic is so important is that the health service spends six times as much for each person over seventy-five as it does for each person aged between sixteen and sixty-five, and it has to spend twenty-six times as much through the personal social services. Coinciding with the health service cutback there is a new squeeze on local government personal social services – the very services which in the past have helped relieve the health service by allowing early discharge of elderly and disabled people from institutional care back to their homes.

For the first time, the government is also intending to cut back on the hitherto steady real-terms increase in financial help given to voluntary organizations. We are witnessing, therefore, a triple blow – reductions in health service planned expenditure and numbers, reductions in the personal social services and reductions in the voluntary services expenditure.

The view of the British Medical Association (BMA) is that this is a 'government blueprint for more private medicine'. Mrs Thatcher would clearly like to introduce a marketplace in health. She dares not do it openly, so she does it by the back door, using financial constraints to debilitate. To reject a marketplace in health and be totally committed to the values and strengths of the National Health Service is characteristic of how the concept of the social market should operate in Britain. While being committed to a market orientation for the economy, one should refuse to place a price on every service, every act and every decision, especially in social policy. The values of the marketplace should not dominate in every sphere of human activity and in particular not within the organization of health care.

There is no need to hang our heads in shame over the NHS, nor are we justified in denigrating it or talking of demolishing it. It should be sustained and defended, not dismantled or dismembered. Over the years it has achieved overwhelming public support for its basic structure; there is also considerable evidence that it is a unifying force across the many divisions within British society.

At the start of the nineteenth century the medical profession, only recently established, was fragmented – neither very well regarded nor highly rewarded – and it would have been hard then to predict its emergence as one of the powerful influences on modern society. In the eighteenth century the patient, as the contractor, had been the dominant figure in the relationship with the doctor, but by the middle of the nineteenth century their roles were reversed. In 1858 Parliament created a single register for all practitioners and a council to coordinate all medical education in the United Kingdom. The growth in the power and the influence of the medical profession in the English-speaking world has been spectacular ever since, starting in Britain and then gathering pace in the United States too.

In 1883 Germany introduced the first national system of compulsory sickness insurance, followed by Austria and Hungary. It developed in Britain in 1911 when David Lloyd George, as the Liberal Chancellor of the Exchequer, started the National Insurance Scheme. After the end of the Second World War the NHS was brought in by the Labour Government against the bitter opposition of most doctors, particularly family practitioners.

It is instructive to recall that in 1971, before state insurance intervened, Canada and the United States spent roughly the same proportion of GNP on health. By 1979 Canada's health spending was 7.2 per cent of GNP, a fall from the figure of 7.5 per cent in 1971, whereas in the United States in 1980 the figure was 9.4 per cent and by 1984 nearer 11 per cent. The Canadian insurance monopoly has an administrative cost of 3 per cent of total health spending, against 15 per cent of expenditure covered by various US private insurance schemes. In England and Wales the total NHS expenditure was initially 4 per cent of GNP and had risen to 5.6 per cent by 1980–81, since when it has been fairly constant. It appears from these figures that where government has some control over expenditure, it is better able to exert some measure of financial restraint. But whether a country spends 5.5 or 7.5 or 11 per cent of their GNP on health, the pressures to increase that percentage – whether demographic, technological or professionally inspired – are little different.

Against such a background it is no longer credible for the medical profession to continue to pretend that they can opt out of the economic choices that are inherent in any health system. The fact is that under different health-care systems, whether privately or publicly provided, the members of the medical profession are now quantifiably major economic decision-makers. In Britain in 1982–3 the average level of resources in the control of a general practitioner or family doctor was £80,000, of which approximately £45,000 was the cost of drugs prescribed, £20,000 remuneration, and £15,000 expenses, including the salaries of staff directly employed. In the same year the average hospital doctor, together with nursing colleagues and hospital staff, controlled £160,000 and the average consultant controlled £530,000, over half a million pounds.

The choices that the medical profession make – supposedly against a background of clinical freedom – have profound influence, because of their economic consequences, on who is treated and how. One study, for instance, in 1977 in the USA showed that to lower the symptom-severity criterion for undertaking an appendicitis operation enough to save one life, it would be necessary to perform so many operations on normal patients that it would cost US $43m and cause a loss of 2,053 person-years in convalescence.

Another study found that in 1968, in Canada, before the introduction of the Medical Care Act, the rates of surgical intervention were 1.8 times higher for men and 1.6 times higher for women in Canada than in England and Wales. Mortality rates were no higher.

There have been many studies on the economics of medical care, assessing the screening of breast cancer, cancer of the cervix and foetal screening, and assessing the costs and benefits of day care versus in-patient care and home care versus hospital care. All the evidence there is suggests that medical need is so large relative to the resources that society is able to provide now, and in the foreseeable future, that we can never hope to meet it completely.

In a zero-price market such as in the British NHS, no financial discipline is automatically exerted on decision-makers to ensure that financial considerations are always taken into account. It is now recognized, however, that the medical practitioner cannot and should not escape some of the disciplines of cost-effectiveness associated with market medicine, even when practising within the structure of public medicine.

Doctors in all health-care systems have to decide which patients to spend most of their time on; what drugs to prescribe; what treatment courses to pursue; the place of treatment and length of stay. Implicit in each decision is the choice to use available resources in one way rather than another. Hospitalizing a patient, for example, usually automatically means that somebody else is excluded from that particular hospital bed. Doctors tend not to think of themselves as economic decision-makers, but care is inevitably restricted by resource constraints in the form of queues, waiting-lists or shortages of medical personnel. It is easier for doctors to criticize the deficiencies of the service, and the overall shortage of resources, than to improve their own deployment of resources and the cost-effectiveness of their health care. The constraint on the total resources available means that doctors acting individually can restrict the clinical freedom of their medical colleagues, nurses and scientists, and also limit the effectiveness of health care for other patients.

The medical profession, regardless of whether they operate in a market or public health-care system, needs to reorientate the content of present medical care to stress the role of the physician in the care of the whole patient. This would mean a radical shift away from a sickness service to a health service, away from the engineering approach to medicine towards the holistic approach, reducing the market element and restoring the social element in medical care. There has already been, in Britain, within the medical profession – without the strong commercialization existing in the United States – a discernible revival of interest in preventative action on health matters. It is conceivable that that shift could be magnified and accelerated in the US by the pressures of corporate medicine. For, in a sense, the very individualism characteristic of the medical profession's sovereignty in the past lends itself to supporting a decentralized philosophy of personal responsibility, self-determination, self-regulation and social accountability. It cannot be assumed that the medical profession, which was for so long opposed to state control, will inevitably continue to support the structure of a market health-care system when that system starts to develop its own controls and to turn in on the very profession that was its greatest proponent.

The good physician never diagnoses or treats any symptom in isolation: the whole person, and their environment, may need just as much attention as their ailment. Doctors know even better than the general public that more medicine does not equal more health. Iatrogenic disease – disease which is caused by doctors – is increasing. The dramatic fall in the death rate during the nineteenth and twentieth centuries, when the reputation of the medical profession soared in the public mind, was not due to miracle medicines but to the improvements in hygiene and public health. The dramatic fall in deaths from tuberculosis *preceded* the discovery of the drugs that killed the tubercle – a fact that was not until recently widely realized outside the medical profession. The killers we all now know are the degenerative diseases, associated with prosperity and progress. The life expectancy of adults in the US has not improved in the thirty-two years from 1950 to 1982, during which national expenditure on medical care rose from \$12bn to over \$275bn. Only 5 per cent of that budget is devoted to health promotion with 95 per cent devoted to disease care. The question for the medical profession in Britain, as elsewhere, is – should it continue to muddle through, preserving the status quo, with perhaps marginal adaptation? Or should it attempt a fundamental rethink?

The extension of community care is not just a financial problem. It is stuck because of frozen attitudes, because we have grown used to mouthing the words community care without matching them with action and generating a welcoming response from the community itself. It is time that we started to talk a different kind of language about community care. We should start talking more about rights and choice. We should be especially wary of monopoly provision where the providers serve those in the community with the least bargaining power. The community are entitled to three choices: public, private and voluntary non-profit-making provision.

The case for a new approach stems from a record of failure over the last fifteen years. The government's document on *Care in the Community* made some useful suggestions but it did not really come to terms with the enormity of the unfilled tasks. Community care in terms of a good standard of service outside large institutions exists at the moment mainly for the elderly and even for them only for the physically disabled rather than the mentally confused.

The worst failure has been in community care for mentally ill people. The number of residential places provided by local authorities has shown little growth since 1976. There has been some increase in the number of day-centre places but there are still many local authorities which do not provide any at all. Support, care and rehabilitation are still mainly from a hospital base.

For mentally handicapped people there has been little progress towards providing opportunities outside hospitals for more severely handicapped adults. Taking hostels and hospitals together, there are now more adults in residential care than in 1971. The reduction in numbers in the large hospitals has been much less than planned in the 1971 White Paper. The record overall, despite some notable exceptions, is poor in terms of quality as well as of quantity. For mentally handicapped people in need of residential care the choice has been a limited one, generally between a place in a hostel or a place in a hospital. The kind of service provided there leaves much to be desired in many cases. The hostels are too large – over 40 per cent of the places have been provided in hostels with more than twenty-five places and the 1979 Report on Mental Handicap Nursing and Care was rightly critical of the care provided in them. The hospitals are staffed mainly by un-qualified staff and there is a great shortage of remedial staff. In 1981 there were only 142 physiotherapists and eighty-three physiotherapy helpers for 43,000 patients. This seems a very poor share, given that the overall number of physiotherapy posts within the NHS totalled almost 7,000. Hospital care is still based on the large geographically isolated institution which makes it very difficult for families to keep in contact. There are many features – not least the excessive influence of medical models of care – which can be explained only in terms of producer interest.

We should look at new ways of extending choice and making it possible for good voluntary groups to take more initiatives. At present voluntary groups find it very difficult to get secure funding for providing services for more handicapped people; these funds tend to be cut off when social services are short of money. At present there is Hobson's choice – the monopoly services or private care in boarding houses and similar places, which is often of a very poor quality. With rate-capping legislation and the pressure on local authority budgets the position is likely to get worse.

The government should take a deliberate decision that the funds available from reducing numbers in hospital should be used to fund many more projects by voluntary non-profit-making organizations who could compete with private and public provision. The handicapped have every bit as much right to choice as anyone else.

Community care for more handicapped people will in the main turn out to be slightly more costly than hospital care. But we need to get away from thinking that the only alternative for the handicapped is institutional state provision or private residential care. Government has to take a deliberate decision to encourage a greater variety of providers. Such mixed provision is the best way of ensuring rights and extending choice for some of those with the least power in our society. Instead of accepting that the future of medical care lies in developing ever larger institutions filled with ever more costly medical technology, is it not time we asked ourselves whether these are the right priorities? Whether it would not be more sensible to redistribute money and redefine values within the health-care budget? The worldwide hospice movement for the care of terminal illness is a remarkable example of a different and viable new pattern of care.

Another important area is preventative action; the degree to which this area has been neglected in the rush towards therapeutic and technological medicine is little short of being a public scandal. The litmus test of whether a government is serious about preventative action on health is how they act over tobacco. It is an incontrovertible fact that cigarette smoking causes lung cancer, chronic bronchitis and coronary artery disease, all now present in the community in epidemic proportions. Beyond the individual level however, smoking affects many non-smokers, who suffer discomfort from cigarette smoke; it brings tragedy to the families of those who die; and it imposes a massive financial burden on the state through the provision of health services and widows' pensions. These dangers were spelt out in the first-ever government publication which was aimed at influencing the general public's attitudes to preventative health measures, *Prevention and Health: Everybody's Business* (1975). It was reiterated in reports to the

House of Commons, in the White Paper *Prevention and Health*, and in a further updated report from the Royal College of Physicians. Sadly, all that has followed has been the usual exhortation, a new duty on cigarettes with a tar yield of over 20mg and a further steep rise in the tax on tobacco. Those addicted to smoking continue to smoke; there is no scientific strategy to help them give up smoking, no serious attempt to change the smoking habits of the young and the increasing number of women who smoke.

In 1984 it is not credible for government to continue to rely on voluntary agreements wrung out of a reluctant tobacco industry. Legislative authority is needed if a serious strategy is to be devised to reduce the harm that tobacco products are causing to health.

In 1975, the government agreed to use the 1968 Medicine Act as part of such a strategy. Section 105 of the Medicine Act has a provision under which Health Ministers might by Order specify a product as subject to all the many different forms of control covered by the Medicine Act. The quickest way to proceed by this method would have been the Affirmative Resolution procedure which theoretically could have become law within sixty days. But this had drawbacks. In Parliament the Joint Select Committee on Statutory Instruments might have challenged the use of the Order, though this was a proper use of the Act. And the industry itself might have used the courts to oppose the measure. The alternative was a one-clause Bill, amending Section 105(1)b of the Medicine Act.

Unfortunately, the decision was not implemented because the Labour government feared too much the effect on voters and the capacity of the industry to generate criticism on the grounds of anxiety about job losses. The arguments about a loss of a specious freedom and lobbyists giving currency to scare-stories about cigarettes being available on prescription only did not help the collective resolve of the government.

The scientific case for specifying tobacco products under the Medicine Act, whether by Order or Amendment, is overwhelming. The use of the 1968 legislation would mean establishing under Section 4 of the Act a specialist committee who would provide expert and authoritative medical and scientific advice on the health risks of tobacco. It has its advantages for the tobacco industry in that they could be fully involved and consulted before any orders or regulations could be made. This procedure already operates with the pharmaceutical industry.

Under Section 62 of the Act, it could be made illegal to sell or import cigarettes with what was deemed to be an excessive tar, nicotine or carbon-monoxide level, or containing any other specified ingredient, provided this was always done on the advice of the Section 4 Committee. Similarly, the industry would be obliged under Part V of the Act to comply with labelling and other requirements imposed on the advice of the Section 4 Committee. And under Part I V of the Act, advertising and promotion of tobacco products could be either banned or controlled. The licensing powers that exist under Part II of the Medicine Act could also be used to cover substitutes or additives.

Obviously the industry will oppose such measures, but it is now diversifying fast into other products, realizing that they cannot go on resisting inevitable change. The Medicine Act is a proven piece of legislation, familiar to both the medical profession and the industry, and sense surely dictates the advantages of using a long complex Act, already on the Statute Book, which has inbuilt safeguards balancing different but legitimate interests, and above all of putting the whole issue on a firm medical and scientific base which takes the issue out of the political arena.

The industry would have an elaborate appeals machinery. The profession would have the opportunity of developing a scientifically based strategy to reduce smoking and minimize some of the worst damage for those who continue to smoke. In a complex field, there would be the opportunity of applying a comprehensive strategy operating not just on price but also on promotion and on the content of cigarettes.

John Stuart Mill argued in the last century, in his essay *On Liberty*, that 'society has no business, as society, to decide anything to be wrong which concerns only the individual', qualifying this with the words 'society cannot be acting wrongly in endeavouring to exclude the influence of solicitations which are not dis-interested'. What in a free and democratic society should be done? We cannot continue to ignore the social evil of tobacco. We ought to be horrified by our sheer negligence when facing such a proven health hazard. The voluntary agreements that have hitherto served as the industry's window-dressing of concern do not begin to grapple with the huge problems that exist. The framework of the Medicine Act offers the basis for a new approach.

But instead of just making an institutional response over preventative measures, whether on tobacco or alcohol, an even more interesting response would be for the medical profession itself to foster changes in public attitudes towards self-help and self-awareness in the field of health care.

To a considerable extent a redistribution of resources is happening already, for medical self-care is part of the self-help, DIY approach to different activities. But it is a real dilemma for the medical profession whether this movement should grow in the teeth of medical hostility, against a background of indifference or in a supportive enthusiastic atmosphere where self-help becomes not just an appendage to modern medicine, but an integral part of it. In a sense this raises the question of the whole relationship between the volunteer and the professional. The voluntary movement was at one time central to the medical-care system. Yet it has been squeezed out initially by the introduction of public provision and more recently by the growth of private provision.

Self-care programmes in the United States have reduced the number of people experiencing diabetic comas and the cost of treating haemophiliacs. On a less sophisticated level we see in Britain Well-Women clinics and the self-help movement progresses from do-it-yourself pregnancy testing to monitoring blood pressure, heart beat and even taking smears. Alcoholics Anonymous, Weightwatchers groups, all flourish as people organize themselves to deal with conditions from schizophrenia to Alzheimer's disease. If the self-help movement is to work with the professional providers of medical care and not be the grit in the system, then the movement needs to be embraced, not shunned; it needs to be seen as an additional resource, not an additional burden. This will require a reorientation of medical attitudes, starting in medical school. It will mean reassessing the role of the community in the development of patterns of medical care, particularly necessary given the demographic pressures of an ageing population, with many living beyond the age of eighty and more people with severe handicaps living longer. It will mean the restoration of the supportive community, where social concern can bear fruit and manifest itself in towns as well as in more integrated rural communities. The traditional moral values of medicine should be a counter-weight to the mechanistic, technological cost-effectiveness of the marketplace.

These are not idealistic political musings in an attempt to define new ways of avoiding finding the financial resources that medicine needs in a modern age. Rather they are an assertion that the true values that underpin the medical profession demand that health promotion and disease prevention are given a new priority and that though it cannot replace technological and therapeutic medicine, it is an all-important complement to it. We should not even attempt to reverse scientific advance or technological progress. Rather we must ensure that a better balance in care is struck; in this way modern health care will achieve its full poten-tial. The holistic approach is not a new-fangled trendy manifesta-tion of quirky cults and way-out opinions. It is the reassertion of the traditional caring values, where a sensitivity to the individuality of the person is a precious part of the practice of the healing profession. The practice of medicine involves the whole person and that has been largely lost sight of in current medical education. We have blurred responsibility for treatment. We have fragmented the method of payment and the responsibility for patient care. In consequence we are in danger of destroying our caring values and purpose.

CHAPTER NINE

European Security Responsibilities

When we get to the point, as we one day will, that both sides know that in any outbreak of general hostilities, regardless of the element of surprise, destruction will be both reciprocal and complete, possibly we will have sense enough to meet at the conference table with the understanding that the era of armaments has ended and the human race must conform its actions to this truth or die.

President Eisenhower, 1956

The vital connection between the political and economic development of Europe and its defence was clearly seen after the Second World War by Winston Churchill and by the founding fathers of the European Community, Jean Monnet and Paul Henri Spaak. The connection was obscured in the 1950s and 1960s by those who posed artificial choices, a European Defence Community – or the Atlantic Alliance? Neutralism or becoming an American satellite? It has long been clear that NATO was insufficient by itself to assure European security and that that needed the political underpinning of the European Community. It is clear too that the painful financial restructuring of the European Community will never come if Britain in particular sees its membership of the European Community on a narrow canvas, divorced from the broader political and social imperatives of European security.

In March 1952, in Lisbon, NATO, in its most important 'Declaration of Aims', made it clear that while it had been forged as a shield against aggression, its first aim was peace and that the partnership between its nations was not for defence alone. The member states in Lisbon 'looked forward to the time when the main energies of NATO could be less concentrated on defence and more fully devoted to cooperation in other fields for the well-being of their peoples and advancement of human progress.'

The Messina Conference in 1955 had as its first essential priority to build up Franco-German understanding, something which all present sensed could never be achieved just within NATO (of which at that stage France was a full participant). Even then people knew Europe needed the wider forum of an economic, trading and political community, but at that time neither British politicians nor the British public would accept the necessary political commitment to European unity. Historians will probably conclude that it was inevitable that the European Community started with only the original six continental countries.

When Portugal and Spain, hopefully in 1986, join the European Community, eleven of NATO's sixteen member states will be political partners in the Community as well as military partners in the North Atlantic Alliance. It is not credible that what will then be over 300 million Europeans, relatively prosperous, technologically highly advanced, wanting greater unity in political, economic, social, trade and industrial matters, can continue to allow their all-important security relationships to be virtually immune from collective European discussion. It no longer reflects the reality of European policies to continue to rely only on ad hoc arrangements for European discussion on security issues. The NATO forum whereby individual member states act separately is inevitably largely dominated by the United States. This automatic American political dominance, justifiable in the aftermath of the Second World War, is no longer underpinned by the weight of their contribution to collective European defence. Nor does it take account of the growing political maturity and independence of the EEC; it has grown not just with prosperity, but in particular with the political self-confidence of West Germany.

European security consciousness even to the point of European defence is not a new concept. It is easy to forget how near continental Europe came to establishing an actual European defence force in the 1950s and how the issue returned in the guise of a multilateral force in the 1960s. The invasion of South Korea on 25 June 1950 resulted in considerable pressure from the United

States for West German rearmament. On 11 August 1950, at the Council of Europe, Winston Churchill, following the lead of Paul Reynaud, formally proposed a motion – which was carried – calling for the formation of a European army under a European minister of defence. In October the French Premier, René Pleven, argued in the National Assembly that it was right that West Germany should share in preparing for the defence of Europe. He stipulated three essential elements: first, the ratification of the Schuman Plan for placing all coal and steel production of France and Germany under a common high authority, which would be open to other European countries; second, the appointment of a European defence minister; and, third, the establishment of a political body to supervise the defence minister's actions. The French National Assembly subsequently approved the Pleven Plan, but the difficulties inherent in creating a European Defence Community (EDC) soon became obvious. First, it was necessary to establish some common ground between the newly established American-dominated NATO and the proposed defence community. Second, a defence community faced the problem of West Germany in relation to the occupying powers and the fundamental changes in the Occupation Statute which would be necessary for West Germany to be able to participate. Finally, before any EDC could be established, the all-important question had to be answered of how to develop financial and political control mechanisms which would effectively integrate a grouping of national armies. The early 1950s was a time of great idealism for the goal of a united Europe. The concept of a united Europe was seen not just from a limited national viewpoint, where short-term economic consequences predominate, but as part of a wider vision. In Paris, on 15 February 1951, Robert Schuman spoke of the attempt to substitute for the very instrument of past struggles 'a common army that will be able to act only in defence of their common civilization'.

These were fine sentiments but slowly in Germany and in France the critics of the EDC gained in strength. In France, where there were genuine fears of German rearmament, the opposition was particularly bitter. Some prominent Europeans opposed the EDC on the grounds that military integration should not precede political integration, and there was also disappointment that the

EDC did not embrace the whole of Europe and particularly Britain. In 1954 the French National Assembly rejected the European Defence Community; this was the start of a persistent and continued refusal by France to accept any significant steps that could impede her independence. The widespread view was that no future progress in the defence field could succeed until there had been a much greater degree of political integration. In 1955 Britain did not even attend the Messina Conference which led to the Treaty of Rome. Then for some years the focus of European political activity was on building the Community of the original six. In June 1962 Harold Macmillan, who was pushing for British entry to the Community, met with General de Gaulle and in the hope of persuading him that Britain would be a good European and not a Trojan Horse for the Americans, indicated that after entry to the Community, Britain would Europeanize her defence to the extent even of a European army and a European deterrent. But de Gaulle, always a bitter critic of the EDC, had no wish to see Britain dilute the Community of Six and was still suspicious of the traditional Anglo-American link. He wanted at least more time to put a distinctive French stamp on the Community and vetoed the British application.

General de Gaulle always rightly saw the politics of nuclear weapons as an area of fundamental importance. It involved for him the prestige and position of France in the world; and it was also a central determinant in his attitude to NATO. Before de Gaulle returned to power, the French had responded to what they saw as an exclusive Anglo-American nuclear club by a decision to build their own isotope separation plant and a commitment to developing their own nuclear weapon capability. At that time France was prepared to involve their European partners. In 1958 Franz-Josef Strauss and Jacques Chaban-Delmas, then Defence Ministers for West Germany and France, entered into negotiations which included Italy for a trilateral agreement, whereby Italy and Germany, in exchange for nuclear information for primarily civil purposes, would contribute to the cost of the French isotope separation plant. These secret negotiations never achieved very much because General de Gaulle unilaterally revoked the military part of the agreement in September 1958. Another chance for wider cooperation was lost when the possibility of the United States providing nuclear propulsion technology for French submarines, specifically offered by John Foster Dulles to de Gaulle in July 1958, also collapsed, when the French decided in March 1959 to refuse to allow their Mediterranean fleet to be on call to NATO in time of war. This followed de Gaulle's 1958 memorandum calling for France, the United States and Britain to join to form a trilateral decision-making body outside NATO.

The next proposal with major European defence implications was for a multilateral force (MLF) first formally put forward by Christian Herter, then Secretary of State in the Eisenhower administration, at a NATO ministerial meeting in December 1960. The only enthusiasts at that time were Germany and Italy. Slowly even their initial enthusiasm for the multilateral force withered away as the detailed problems of how to organize control procedures became more and more complex. The Soviet Union's opposition to the concept of the multilateral force was deep-seated, based on a fear of nuclear technology being made available to the Germans, possibly leading either to a German national nuclear deterrent or to close collaboration with the French. This was a prospect that seemed real enough following the signing of the Franco-German pact in January 1963, and was greatly enhanced by the well-advertised German support for the MLF concept.

In Britain, opposition focused on the prospect of a 'German finger on the nuclear trigger', and there was little enthusiasm for the MLF in the British armed services. The problems were easy to identify, but the will to come to grips with developing adequate control mechanisms, for either an MLF or a multinational defence force, was lacking. Eventually the MLF proposal encountered a succession of political and military difficulties. General de Gaulle was always opposed and used the Common Market tariff negotiations to exert pressure on Chancellor Erhard. In November 1964, the new Labour government in Britain produced a proposal for an Atlantic nuclear force which was essentially a political initiative aimed at destroying the MLF. Discussions on majority voting, multiple vetoes and double-key arrangements always foundered on the problem of persuading national governments and national parliaments to give up control over what they considered to be a key area of policy. Some countries were very reluctant to accept any American veto, preferring the force to be entirely European. Finally, all hopes of any agreement were destroyed in February 1966 when France announced that they were pulling out of NATO's integrated command structure.

Against such a complicated and fraught history it would be an act of political masochism to embark again on the pursuit of a specifically European defence force. It would not only be doomed to fail but it would also be a dangerous folly. It is not in Europe's interests to set out to design a self-contained European defence structure without the United States, in an attempt to match the Warsaw Pact. But we should not ignore the slow but steady progress that has been made in developing a European security identity. The European Community under Political Cooperation has taken a position on the SALT (Strategic Arms Limitation Treaty) negotiations and on the UN Special Sessions on Disarmament, and there has been a growing exchange across the interface between the EEC and NATO. It would be going down a dangerous blind alley to continue into the 1990s without building up at a rather faster pace than hitherto the capacity to develop a specifically European defence and disarmament policy to work with and influence US policy within NATO. Many Europeans do not yet realize that we in Europe now provide 91 per cent of the ground forces, 80 per cent of the main battle tanks and combat aircraft and two thirds of major ships in the European area of the Alliance. Europe has been reluctant to assert itself politically on security issues and has allowed an unwarranted imbalance to develop in the negotiating framework for the disarmament and arms-control arrangements that critically affect Europe. The Americans negotiate for NATO on intermediate European-nuclear-force levels as well as on strategic systems. The Soviets argue with some logic for the inclusion of British and French strategic weapons systems in arms control talks, yet it is we Europeans who have accepted that the talks should be limited to only US and Soviet participation. France and Britain resist any discussion, more out of fear of being asked to cut below what they see as a minimum deterrent than because there is no appropriate forum for such discussions involving their weapon systems.

Western Europe has tolerated a 10:1 imbalance in transatlantic trade in defence equipment despite the fact that our own manufacturing industry has the skills and capacity to match those of the US. On economic and trading grounds alone, the European Community can no longer stand aside from this imbalance. There is an urgent need for far greater European coordination in the defence procurement field; otherwise we will be accepting US domination in a sector of sophisticated technology well into the next century. The Independent European Programme Group was established to involve the French but has never been given the political backing it requires.

The imperative now is to consciously develop a European identity firmly within NATO, to cover both conventional and nuclear defence, along with disarmament policy. It is no longer credible to argue that such a development will weaken the American commitment or create strains within NATO. The nature, if not the content, of the American commitment has been changing. The strains exist already. Different perceptions started for Britain at the time of Suez in 1956. After the October 1962 Cuban missile crisis when, in Kruschev's emotive phrase, 'the smell of burning hung in the air', Europeans heaved a sigh of relief that they could still, even after the abortive Bay of Pigs invasion, trust President Kennedy to handle a critical US–Soviet issue with great restraint. Most Europeans felt then that our security was in a 'safe pair of hands'. There have been too many incidents since, worldwide, for Europeans to feel the same trust in subsequent US Presidents. In the late 1970s, in Africa, when dealing with the Kolwezi incident in Zaïre, the Somalian invasion of the Ogaden and more recently in Chad, Europe had an important influence on US policy. In the Middle East the European influence has been much less. The lesson of the multilateral peacekeeping force in the Lebanon is that France, Italy and Britain should have insisted on having a far greater diplomatic influence, particularly in the handling of Syria. More seriously, western Europe differed from America in their perception of Soviet motives in invading Afghanistan after the coup which threatened Soviet influence. In the main the European members of NATO saw Soviet intervention as more defensive than expansionist – still indefensible but less threatening. We differed too in our appreciation of Soviet involvement in the military clampdown in Poland where the US correctly faced up to the reality of the Kremlin's involvement.

One does not have to succumb to the predominant anti-American European mood triggered off by some of President Reagan's rhetoric to conclude sadly that the post-war absolute European confidence in the US has gone. Many Europeans who are totally convinced of NATO's value now openly express their anxiety about US decision-making.

The nature of the US nuclear guarantee for Europe has always been subject to anxious discussion. The European members of NATO have ambivalent and often contradictory feelings and the responsibility for this unease is shared. Over the neutron bomb and over theatre-nuclear-weapon modernization it has to be admitted that most European leaders wanted deployment but preferred the Americans to take the responsibility for implementation. The Europeans were able to agree at the NATO Heads of Government meeting in 1978 to increase by 3 per cent per year in inflation-proof terms its spending on conventional forces for NATO, but they nevertheless still hesitate over reducing NATO's reliance on the early use of nuclear weapons, fearing the effects of a conventional battle on their continent. Europeans see disarmament negotiations as a way of reducing the danger of nuclear conflict and yet are not prepared to make a distinctive impact on these negotiations.

West Germany in particular is hesitant to involve itself in nuclear defence policy given that they have forsworn becoming a nuclear-weapon state and adhere firmly to their commitments under the Non Proliferation Treaty; they have fought shy of dual key on Pershing II and cruise missiles, though they have accepted it on existing Lance and Pershing missiles.

France supports NATO's decision to deploy cruise missiles and Pershing II. They plan to replace their Pluton missiles, which have a range of 165 km, with Hades, which has a range of around 350 km and is capable of reaching East Germany from French territory. They are adapting their conventional-force structure to make them more mobile and thereby more capable of providing early reinforcement in the Federal Republic of Germany. These developments carry important implications for Europe's defence policy and reflect underlying military trends that western Europe cannot push aside and have already led to much greater Franco-German security cooperation.

In Britain the post-war all-party consensus over defence went when the Labour Party finally endorsed the full unilateral nuclear disarmament position. Yet the objective, political and strategic considerations continue to reinforce the view that Britain should remain as long as financially feasible a nuclear-weapon state, that there would be serious implications for the Federal Republic of Germany if Britain were to abandon its present role as a nuclear-weapon state and that France – outside NATO – should not be the only western European nuclear-weapon state. A British and French minimum nuclear capacity is needed within Europe, not as an independent force but as a last-resort safeguard for Europe if a western European defence identity is to be credible and if European relations on nuclear questions with the United States are to achieve a better balance, with Europe influencing US strategic thinking.

These are important policy decisions which should be faced up to in Britain as Europeans, not just as an individual member state within NATO. It is an extraordinary manifestation of Britain's overall decline and loss of confidence that few are prepared systematically to expose the 1984 defence position of the government to critical scrutiny. A strange silence has descended; it is as if no one can quite believe that after the victory in the southern Atlantic we are witnessing a second attempt to slash our conventional defence forces and in particular the Royal Navy. The first cutbacks announced in 1981 had at least an intellectual basis and the sums added up, whereas the 1984 announcement of a cutback in 1986 has no intellectual basis. It is also clear that the figures do not even add up.

The 1984 forward estimate for total defence expenditure (including the Falklands) for the years 1986–7 shows a real-terms increase of 0.5 per cent. That was based on a 3 per cent inflation rate in 1986–7, which most people believe to be wildly unrealistic. If inflation in 1986–7 rises over 3.5 per cent there will be an absolute reduction in defence spending. If Falklands expenditure is excluded, even on existing inflation assumptions there will be zero real growth in defence spending in 1986/7 and beyond. No amount of management efficiency economies can disguise the extent of the planned erosion of our conventional fighting capability.

The 1984 Defence Estimates put the total cost of the Trident programme at £8,729m, based on an exchange rate of $1.53, as outlined in the earlier Public Expenditure White Paper. What is sometimes forgotten, however, is the fact that because some 45 per cent of the estimate (£3,928m) represents spending in dollars, exchange-rate fluctuations can alter the total cost substantially. As the pound moves down against the dollar the Trident programme already costs, depending on the rate, £400–500m more than allowed for in the Defence Estimates. This may be a conservative estimate. The Centre for Defence Studies at Aberdeen University forecasts a figure for the programme of £11,500m at 1984/5 prices and exchange rates.

The escalating cost of Trident, particularly the escalation in the cost of building the boats, following the US experiences, promises to place a crippling squeeze on the growth of Britain's conventional defence equipment budget. This is well illustrated by the fact that our naval general-purpose combat forces in 1984–5 will receive only a 1 per cent real terms increase from the commitment made in 1983–4. The forward outlook is far worse. The Royal Navy has been given the impression that the 1981 cutbacks have been reversed. The force of three aircraft carriers has been restored – the government previously opted for two. The amphibious assault ships are to be kept. *HMS Endurance* remains in the Southern Atlantic. The frigate and destroyer fleet will still go down from fifty-nine to fifty; but eight ships that according to the 1981 plan were to be held in reserve will now be put on full duty, yet without any increase in previously planned manpower. Overall, Royal Navy manpower levels in the early 1990s are to be 11,000 less than in 1981.

The facts clearly show that if the Trident programme is maintained it can only be at the expense of the conventional forces. Instead of the new equipment – in 1981 the government promised to strengthen the weapons mix of the Royal Navy, we will be going back to the old recipe of more surface hulls but less modern missile equipment, fewer nuclear-powered Hunter Killer submarines and less new construction, heading in general to an ageing fleet. This is the wrong policy choice, for Britain and for NATO. There is no merit in posing an artificial choice between keeping the British Army of the Rhine or maintaining a maritime role. In establishing the balance between our navy, army and air-force contribution to NATO, we cannot deny our history and our geography. We are an island race, not a nation hewn out of a continent; we have a long tradition of blue-water diplomacy. The horizons of that diplomacy have shortened, but we should not see our Europeanism as an exclusive relationship, for it is necessary for Europe itself to look outwards to the world. It should be the special British contribution to Western Europe to maintain a strong navy even if it means we cannot preserve an equal three-part balance in the shape of our armed services.

Britain is not going to be able to improve its conventional defence contribution to NATO without new thinking. In 1984 we are already having to divert a substantial sum to the maintenance of Fortress Falklands. The government's refusal to enter into serious negotiations by agreeing to discuss Argentina's sovereignty claims is a folly; we will have to negotiate eventually, but even an optimist cannot be sure of the Argentinians being ready to reach a compromise on some mechanism for UN Security Council Trusteeship or shared sovereignty, without many years of negotiating elapsing. The cost of maintaining the Fortress Falklands policy will be high. The government's own estimates reveal that spending on the Falklands will be running at £684m in 1984/5, £552m in 1985/6 and £450m in 1986/7. These are large amounts, which will be diverted from the conventional defence budget.

The problem of achieving the right balance between conventional forces and nuclear forces is not new. Duncan Sandys, as Minister of Defence in the late 1950s, formally tilted the balance to rely on nuclear deterrence rather than conventional defence, but it had been happening for some time before this. Britain after the Korean war dropped its conventional armed force numbers, ended national service and, on the basis of a 'bigger bang for a buck', relied too much on nuclear weapons. Initially the conventional wisdom was 'mutual assured destruction', which then moved perilously close to adopting a battlefield nuclear war fighting strategy. We who reject the NATO strategy of 'early use' of nuclear weapons when facing a conventional surprise attack have a particular need to grapple with ways of improving our conventional defence. Some have attempted to shortcut the question of manpower by advocating a return to conscription with an opt-out provision for community service instead. They cite, not altogether unfairly, the fact that such a system exists in France, Germany, Belgium, Denmark, Greece, Holland, Norway, Portugal, Spain, Italy, Sweden and Switzerland. But almost everyone who has looked at this as a solution for Britain has been bound to conclude that there are formidable obstacles. First and foremost there have been very considerable gains from providing a professional armed service, even though it is very expensive. One only needs to point to the resolution and self-control that they have exhibited under intense provocation in Northern Ireland and to their professionalism in the Falkland Islands.

There are large numbers of highly trained servicemen in the Warsaw Pact countries, but improving NATO's conventional defence on the central front depends, not on matching Warsaw Pact forces man for man, but on precision-guided conventional munitions, better equipment and improved airlift capacity for greater mobility. We need more men, however, in the defence of the United Kingdom at or after the time of mobilization, when our regular and reserve forces move to the continent. The new concept of home defence has been inspired largely in response to the public disclosure of the existence of 'Spetsinaz' groups of highly trained English-speaking Soviet forces that would infiltrate the UK at times of tension and prior to the commencement of hostilities. The presence of even around 1,000 such people close to mobilization would present a tremendous challenge to the stability of the UK, and it is a serious question as to how this new factor should be counteracted.

In the absence of agreement in the Mutual Balanced Force Reduction Talks, Britain ought to consider a modest increase in its front-line highly trained mobile reserve, particularly for the army. We must consider expanding the numbers of people available in emergency, looking at ways of complementing the Territorials, remembering that a first-line Territorial soldier costs £12,000, as against a regular soldier at £20,000 a year. Imaginative schemes of one-year full-time service with a seven-year, initially intensive, part-time training commitment to the mobile reserve, declining to a commitment to home defence, need to be considered. This would fit more easily into the career pattern of young people than the minimum three-year full-time commitment. The obstacle to a shorter full-time period of service lies in the attitude of the services. The highly trained reserve would need only a small fraction of the million men and 800,000 women who would be eligible under a national call-up. Even those needed for a very ambitious home-defence effort would be considerably less. It would be absurd therefore to conscript for the armed services when the demand was for only a small proportion of the total. In any case, compulsory national service ended in 1962 and we cannot simply reverse the trends of the less hierarchical, less deferential, more informal and disaggregated society which we have developed. If we can develop the Volunteer Community Service Scheme outlined in Chapter 7, there is no reason why it should not offer also a one-year forces training scheme, such as has been described, directed more to home defence than to the Territorial mobile reserve, since guarding the community is part of serving the community.

The government's policy of continuing with Trident means in three or five years' time there will not be enough resources to maintain the present Hunter Killer submarine build rate, to carry on with the missile re-equipment programme and Saxon armoured vehicles, and to finance in full the new agile combat aircraft programme.

Even if we sacrifice, as we should, the Trident programme, we cannot earmark the moneys that are saved for the Health Service or for education, much though one would wish that to happen. In the absence of agreement on mutual force reductions, money will be needed to improve Britain's conventional defence forces – something which we must do if we are to raise the nuclear threshold in Europe.

The government pretends, in defence of Trident, that it represents the minimum size necessary to provide a credible and effective deterrent. They claim they have no intention of increasing the capability of the force beyond the minimum. But this is nonsense. Trident represents a big increase in terms of missile numbers and nuclear megatonnage as compared to Polaris; it represents an increase in megatonnage for each submarine from 38 megatons to 214 and an increase in the number of warheads on each missile from three, multiple but not independently targetable, to eight, independently targetable. The government claim that Trident will only absorb 3 per cent of the total defence budget and 6 per cent of the total equipment budget over the next fifteen years, but this ignores the fact that in the late 1980s the government is planning no increase in defence spending, at a time when Trident expenditure will represent nearly 7.5 per cent of the total military spending and 15–20 per cent of the capital spending.

We must ask what is to replace the Trident programme if it is halted. To refuse to grapple with this is to choose to go into the next century with no nuclear deterrent for the United Kingdom. The key to the answer lies in the United States Tomahawk cruise missile programme: Tomahawk missiles are being fitted to US nuclear-powered submarines; some nuclear-armed Tomahawk missiles became operational in submarines in the middle of 1984. The Americans have implemented this programme because they believe that Tomahawk is an effective weapon system. Replacing the Polaris system with Tomahawk would fit easily into a British minimum-deterrent strategy. This would not have to be done until the end of the 1990s, for even now the last Polaris boats are planned to remain in service until 1997.

Tomahawk is not the most sophisticated deterrent system. It is not as good technically or strategically as the Trident system and it would be foolish to try to pretend otherwise. However, bearing in mind the developing capacity to shoot down missiles in space, the ballistic Trident missile system may not prove as advantageous in the next century as many thought. The submarine-launched cruise missile is a cheap deterrent because it can be fired from a conventional torpedo tube in existing SSNs. Only eight missiles are being fitted initially to submarines of the United States Navy. There will later be an extra twelve with vertical launch, to make twenty in all. Eight could be deployed routinely in our existing SSNs and considerably more at times of heightened political tension. It is questionable whether, for a minimum deterrent, Britain needs to be on continuous specially designated deterrent patrols. As long as some submarines are submerged at times of tension that should suffice. The cost will be about $1.2m per missile in 1982 prices. The programme's further costs would depend on whether the SSN build rate was increased. The maximum initial deployment would need to be about 100 missiles, and would cost about one eighth of the present cost of the Trident programme. Alternatively, we could purchase more missiles and incur extra refitting charges and also increase the SSN build rate. The government says that there is no alternative to Trident. We have heard that cry before in other policy areas. There is an alternative, and more and more senior armed service men are realizing the overall consequences for the defence budget of going ahead with the Trident programme.

Defence and disarmament are key issues not just for the NATO member states but for the international standing of the European Community. Responsibility in these areas involves hard practical choices going to the root of our security and Western Europe's relations with bordering countries like East Germany and Czechoslovakia, other Warsaw Pact states like Poland, Hungary and Romania, and even Yugoslavia, outside the Warsaw Pact. The to-ing and fro-ing of East–West relations has increasingly hinged on the Jekyll-and-Hyde nature of the detente process. Competition and cooperation, both inherent in detente, have increasingly vied with each other. Differing perceptions were always acknowledged. The differences were tolerable as long as East and West were determined never to make the process of detente itself so distasteful as to make it worth the other's while to opt out completely. In the early 1980s we came close to the point where the level of confrontation was so high that the structure of detente itself was threatened. Since 1976, when President Ford stopped using the term detente in his election campaign, many NATO members have been searching for another word; only the Soviets have clung both to the term and their concept of what it means. The paradox that is rarely faced is that as contact and communication grows, detente heightens competition between the communist and democratic way of life in East and West. It is because East and West have failed to grapple more openly with this paradoxical development that detente is now endangered.

The complexity of detente means that it must be assessed at many different levels. It represents a coalescence of differing strands. The skill in managing the process of detente is to blend the elements of confrontation and cooperation in its constituent parts. Initially, political dialogue and military vigilance were its main constituents, but it then widened out through cultural links and ideological debate. All of these constituents have the potential for instability developing within them but perhaps none more so than the ideological debate. Here the tempo of language and expectation have recently diverged to a worrying level and at far too rapid a rate. When Mr Andropov said 'a struggle is under way for the minds and hearts of billions of people on the planet, and the future of mankind depends, to a considerable extent, on the outcome of this ideological struggle', he was not saying anything new. President Nixon never had any doubt about the nature of the ideological struggle when, in May 1972 in Moscow, he and Brezhnev signed the first article of the document on the 'Basic Principles of Relations between the USA and the USSR', perhaps the high-water mark of the relationship between the two countries. That document said that:

The USA and the USSR will proceed from the common determination that in the nuclear age there is no alternative to conducting our mutual relations on the basis of peaceful coexistence. Differences in ideology and in the social systems of the USA and the USSR are not obstacles to the bilateral development of normal relations based on the principles of sovereignty, equality, non-interference in internal affairs, and mutual advantage.

The inevitability of the struggle between East and West was soon confirmed by Brezhnev, in December 1972, when he said:

the world outlook of socialism and capitalism are opposite and irreconcilable. But we will strive to direct its historically inevitable struggle into a channel which poses no threat of wars, dangerous conflicts and an uncontrolled arms race.

What was new about the 1980s was not any substantial change in the nature of the ideological struggle, but the hyperbole of language in which senior figures on both sides started to conduct their relations. This preceded the Korean airline massacre – though that itself raised it to new heights. President Reagan equated the Soviet Union with evil. Vice-President Bush, in returning from Romania and Hungary, chose Vienna in which to denounce East Germany, Bulgaria and Czechoslovakia. The speech, ill-judged in both venue and content, said that the US would not 'reward closed societies and belligerent foreign policies'. Some of the European members of NATO found it difficult to square those sentiments with the renewal of Article II of the United States–Soviet grain sales executive agreement, which prohibited the US from exercising 'any discretionary authority available to it under United States law to control exports of commodities purchased for supply to the USSR'. It was absurd for the United States in the light of this to ask Europe to limit high technology sales, even if unrelated to military application to the USSR. Mr Andropov then accused US leaders of 'what almost amounts to obscenities alternating with hypocritical preaching about morals and humanism'. Mrs Thatcher responded to what she interpreted as a 'challenge – I accept it and I do so with the confidence, which Winston Churchill would have shared, that in this battle we in the West hold the cards.' Politicians who invoke Winston Churchill should not forget that the title of his 1946 Fulton speech with its most quoted passage on the Iron Curtain was 'The Sinews of Peace' and it called for a 'settlement' with the Soviet Union. The problem about megaphonic diplomacy is that one acrimonious public exchange begets another. There is no evidence that western public opinion needs alerting to the nature of communism. Frightening the public can weaken, not stiffen, resolve. The effect on the Soviets of turning up the megaphone is to induce a virulent playback from their propaganda bank. The end result is predictable, a dialogue of the deaf. We should negotiate with the Russians at all levels at all times and on all subjects.

We also need to ponder the nature of our relationship with the USSR with more realism. Europe since 1945 has been spared war but has experienced continued division, tension and suppression. The two superpowers remain inviolate within their own territory. The competition for influence, power and ideology has taken place within the eastern and western European nations. It is a solidly based assumption that neither Moscow nor Washington has ever, throughout this period, contemplated invasion. Unlike Berlin in the 1930s, there have been fortunately no serious political leaders in either capital who have dreamt of their form of communism or their form of democracy being imposed by military force. The reasons for this are many and varied, and do not solely, or even partially, rest, as some simplistically assume, on the existence of nuclear weapons. The human horror of war, the physical exhaustion after the devastation of two world wars and the innate caution of the two predominant cultures have been powerful factors for stability. Detente has, paradoxically, opened up a grey area in relationships between the countries of eastern and western Europe as the Iron Curtain which so concerned Churchill in 1946 has been slowly and hesitantly raised. As we began to trade with each other, as families that were split began to reunite across the Curtain's divide, as the cultural links were restored, tensions began to develop, as we consciously or subconsciously began to feel we could influence each other's ideological assumptions. We have explored each other's tolerance limits; the important thing is not to exceed them, for it is then that we risk war.

In a sense, the shattering of hopes in the West in 1981 over the suppression of Solidarity in Poland was greater than after Czechoslovakia in 1968. In the 1950s and 1960s there were few hopes to shatter, expectations were low. The 1975 Helsinki Final Act was meant to mark the end of such brutalizing events as the risings in Hungary in 1956 and in Czechoslovakia in 1968. In 1981 over Poland we expected restraint; yet had detente not existed and had the Soviets not wished to maintain it, we could have seen repeated the same brutal and overt Soviet suppression. Instead we witnessed the covert masterminding of Polish martial law. Too many in the West chose to ignore the Soviet role, even to the extent of seeing General Jaruzelski as a Tito-like figure. To a very limited extent, the Soviets showed more sensitivity to the impact of their actions on the West in Europe in 1981 than they had in 1979 over Afghanistan. There they paid the heaviest price in their relations with the non-aligned world. Over Poland they assessed the West's likely response from their point of view correctly. The graduated pressure gave us in Western Europe room for an accommodation which we too readily took. Who can doubt the reason? Any economic or trade sanctions we applied against the Soviet Union would have hurt in terms of jobs lost, orders forgone, profits reduced. We backed off imposing sanctions that had any real domestic cost, whether refusing to reschedule debt repayments, postponing the European gas pipeline or cancelling US grain sales. The West was loud on rhetoric, and none were louder than President Reagan and Mrs Thatcher. Yet our actions by contrast were infirm and hesitant. The process of detente survived and, from their different standpoints, the Soviets modified the action they took within Poland, and the US and western Europe modified the reaction they made to the events in Poland. Both felt constrained, and a key constraining factor was the economic and trading links that the detente process had forged.

There is little doubt that the same process of modification has influenced both countries in the way they handled the Inter-mediate Nuclear Forces (INF) talks in relation to the Federal Republic of Germany. Both wanted to be seen to have negotiated reasonably by East and West Europeans, particularly the West Germans.

One of the most sensitive and difficult areas in East–West relations is the extent to which Washington or Moscow believe, as detente in Europe progresses, that they can split off eastern Europe from the Soviets or western Europe from the Americans. The sober liberal view in the West, as opposed to the strident conservative view, is to be rather dismissive of such a pos-sibility – to believe the prospect too fanciful, too remote for any such suggestion to be given serious consideration in either the East or the West. Though the technocrats, military or political, charged with strategy in their respective capitals may not give such destabilizing a high priority, some western politicians do. What the politicians in Moscow think is unclear – the evidence is contradictory. What is more important, therefore, is not what action the political leaders in Moscow or Washington plan for themselves but their reaction to what they perceive as the plans of the others. In both capitals, at different times, political leaders recently appear to have responded to events by attributing more sinister objectives to their political counterparts in the other country; the mistakes both the superpowers have made in recent years have been rooted in ideology. The character of their top political leaders has also been more ideological, the readiness to compete greater, the will to cooperate less. This means that, if we are to avoid a serious miscalculation in the next few years, we must learn from the immediate past.

A profound tactical blunder was made by the US when in March 1977 in Moscow, in their first substantive SALT negotiating meet-ing with the Soviets, they put forward their comprehensive deep-cuts proposal, a mistake compounded by President Carter's insistence on spelling out their negotiating position to the UN General Assembly. Back-channel diplomacy was being replaced by podium diplomacy. The Soviets felt the Vladivostok framework was being unilaterally abandoned. Yet when Cyrus Vance, who had privately opposed the new US negotiating position, put down at the same time a fall-back proposal accepting the Vladivostok ceiling but deferring the cruise missile and Backfire issues, why did Andrei Gromyko still respond irrationally and emotionally? Instead of picking up the second proposal the Soviets denounced the whole initiative in strident terms – it was a major setback to detente in general and arms control in particular. The reason was probably neither just President Carter's letter to Andrei Sakharov nor the high US human rights profile, though they contributed. It was the deep Soviet suspicion of the ideological motivation of the Carter administration. Time and time again in 1977 in conversation with Gromyko and with Brezhnev in Moscow they returned to the suspicion about American motives in relation to eastern Europe. Throughout Carter's presidency, while acknowledging the sincerity of Cyrus Vance, they read into every action or reaction of the administration a readiness to destabilize ideologically what they saw as the mutual gains stemming from the Nixon–Kissinger–Ford era.

The next issue which had deep repercussions in terms of European attitudes to nuclear weapons was the manufacture of the neutron bomb. The technology had been around since the 1960s but it became a public issue in June 1977. Setting aside military arguments, its manufacture was a deeply sensitive issue because in all logic its deployment would increase the credibility of a threat to use battlefield nuclear weapons. This went to the core of European arguments about the nuclear threshold and battlefield nuclear war fighting. The Soviets saw an obvious propaganda opening, the potential to drive a wedge into public opinion in NATO countries, and they exploited it whenever they could. Those of us who believe that battlefield nuclear weapons are already dangerous and should be removed argued against the neutron bomb – it was not only the opponents of all nuclear weapons who raised criticisms. When, in April 1978, Carter announced he was deferring production, he sadly got no plaudits. Western Europe, which was divided on the issue of deployment, somewhat _ynically became united about the damage to US credibility in not pushing ahead. The Soviets won a propaganda advantage and gave no credit to Carter for any easing in East–West tensions. In the aftermath, the US felt it necessary to reassert their leadership within NATO and in consequence went along more readily than they would otherwise have done with Europe's wish for theatre-nuclear-weapon modernization. The US also wrongly took more seriously than hitherto the German Chancellor Helmut Schmidt's emphasis on the European strategic balance as distinct from the global balance. In short, the whole episode was a self-inflicted wound and the resultant mess a memory which haunts NATO still. One consequence is that the intermediate weapon deployment pattern is now primarily a political decision. It cannot be seen just as a question of tactical or military utility.

From 1978 onwards, negotiating hurdles continued to be erected by both sides. The Soviets pushed ahead with SS-20 deployment despite being warned about Western concern. US anxiety about the Soviet large missiles with silo-busting potential – and thereby first-strike potential – grew. SALT II's detailed negotiations went on for far too long. With momentum lost and a Cuban scare story, it disappeared into the Congressional sand. The Comprehensive Test Ban (CTB) negotiations, initially so promising, were put on the back burner by the US in 1978, to follow after SALT. Also, the Soviet Union inexplicably threw a spanner into the CTB negotiating position by an unreal demand that Britain should, like the US and the Soviet Union, have twelve seismic stations on its territory. The December 1979 NATO double decision to prepare to deploy and to negotiate was made in the context of modernizing existing nuclear weapons. Though choosing somewhat surprisingly the highest range of deployment options prepared by the High Level Working Group (HLG), NATO did not at that time believe in matching every Soviet SS-20. Since western Europe thought it necessary to replace Pershing I and ageing nuclear aircraft irrespective of SS-20 deployment, to ensure the credibility of the US nuclear guarantee, they could never have endorsed the zero option as anything other than an initial negotiating tactic. It has never been explained why Pershing II's range was extended so much beyond that of Pershing I and why the HLG options for sea- and air-based cruise missiles were totally discarded in favour of ground-launched cruise. The Afghanistan invasion then totally soured relations with the US and led to an emotional overreaction from Carter, who seemed to have suddenly discovered Soviet ideological ruthlessness. The inevitable failure to ratify SALT II, to which the intermediate missile negotiations had been linked, followed, although fortunately President Reagan has kept US nuclear weapons within the SALT II limits. The long delay in establishing the INF talks, during which SS-20 deployment built up, led to the tabling by the US of the unreal zero option which the Soviet Union would have been, in their own interests, wise to accept. The continued Soviet refusal to dismantle SS-20s, their Asian deployment and the Soviet insistence on counting in the French and British nuclear weapons were all factors that contributed to the INF deadlock. The Soviet position over the British and French nuclear forces has a certain logic, but their insistence on including them in the INF talks does not. The Soviets would have a better case for arguing for them to be in the Strategic Arms Reduction Talks (START), particularly since it was the USSR who previously argued that Polaris should be taken into account in fixing SALT levels. Polaris certainly formed part of the background to the SALT II negotiation even though no declared number was formally allocated.

The critical moment over INF came in 1982 when Paul Nitze, the US Ambassador to the talks, and the Soviet Ambassador took their now famous 'walk in the woods' together. Here at last was the bold imaginative step forward which could have broken and still could break the deadlock. No Pershing IIs to be deployed at all, reduced deployment of cruise matched by destruction of some SS-20s. The exact arithmetic was not at that stage as crucial as the shape of the package. Its rejection, first in the Kremlin, then in Washington, was a double blow. The initiative by the negotiators unfortunately came at the wrong time. The US were still fixed on the zero option and the Soviets still felt they could force NATO to make no intermediate missile deployments. History may judge it as an arms control opportunity lost on the same scale as the proposed MIRV moratorium in the late 1960s. But this time the issues do not just affect the superpowers' strategic systems. It is the whole future of European security that is at stake. Now is the time when stern Europe's voice must be raised to insist that the 'walk in the woods' formulation is not lost, but retained, preferably by negotiation, alternatively by NATO imposing it through deploying only cruise and not Pershing missiles. This is particularly so now that the Soviets' crude political attempts to wield a veto on NATO's right to deploy any intermediate missiles have been beaten and the initial deployment of the missiles has been made in Britain, Germany and Italy.

Following the Soviet walk-out from the INF talks in November 1983 the Soviets have not shifted from their absolutist position that in exchange for a substantial reduction in SS-20s, there should be no cruise or Pershing II deployment. In private, however, the Soviets have all along made it clear that they fear Pershing II most for its penetrability and short flight time. They are probably exaggerating their concern, and interestingly they have publicly carefully linked both weapons as equally unacceptable.

Sensing that any deployment would cause internal dissension within NATO countries, the Soviets were unwilling to undercut domestic pressures by agreeing a package which involved them in underwriting NATO deployment, however limited. The US for their part waited far too long to indicate that INF could take into account some of their nuclear carrying aircraft. The French and British could have helped to defuse the Soviet position by showing a greater readiness to put their nuclear submarines into an appropriate negotiating forum.

It is important if the INF talks are to restart or resume within the START forum that we Europeans should develop with the US the sort of final negotiating position which we can not only implement if there is no agreement but will also be judged as reasonable by a broad band of European public opinion. We are dealing almost entirely with a political and not a military problem. For us the all-important question is how to ensure the collective cohesion of NATO. If the negotiations fail in 1985, NATO will be justified in some further deployment, particularly if there has been a pause to allow the Soviet Union to return to the negotiating table. Cruise missiles in Britain should however be dual key.

Though cruise missiles have dominated the nuclear debate in Britain and in Europe over recent years, it is not unreasonable to ask why so little has been done to eliminate the approximately

7,000 short-range battlefield or tactical nuclear weapons in Europe on the NATO side. In the late 1970s they consisted of aerial bombs, artillery rounds, atomic land missiles, short-range missiles and air-defence missiles on land and at sea around Europe. They are easily the most dangerous trigger for nuclear war.

In December 1979 NATO made a unilateral decision to reduce battlefield nuclear weapons by 1,000 and then, on 28 October 1983, to withdraw another 1,400 warheads during the next few years. But the military significance of these decisions was minimal since many of the weapons to be taken out – such as the land mine and the Nike-Hercules anti-aircraft missiles – were obsolete, and the absence of any land corridor devoid of deployment means that the dangerous justification for their deployment is still being accepted.

The importance of concentrating on this aspect of nuclear weapons is that more people need to be convinced and, even more important, to act on the fears expressed in an important speech made in 1979 by Lord Mountbatten. Speaking as a military man, he said, 'I cannot imagine a situation in which nuclear weapons would be used as battlefield weapons without the conflagration spreading.' Until that view becomes even more widely held and is formally endorsed by NATO, we will not even begin to move towards a strategy of no-first-use of nuclear weapons. It is the hinge issue which precedes all other action, whether for those who argue we should be developing a non-provocative 'Just Defence' policy or simply for those who argue we should be spending more on conventional defence to reinforce the existing patterns.

The reason why nearly 5,000 battlefield nuclear weapons are still deployed by NATO is that not all of NATO's military commanders accept that using battlefield nuclear weapons would lead to an escalation of the conflict. They also believe that its deterrent effect is valuable in dissuading the Soviets from massing their conventional forces in East Germany prior to an attack. It is, they argue, an absolute precondition of holding a Soviet attack using conventional troops that the Warsaw Pact is inhibited from massing their conventional forces in such numbers that NATO could never hold a concentrated attack across a narrow front. To the extent that this argument has any validity the intermediate missiles, Pershing or cruise, which are stationed well back from the

line, could be invoked to threaten second-echelon targets in
astern Europe. At least the removal of battlefield weapons and
reliance on intermediate weapons instead means that the decision
to use them need not be taken in the first twenty-four hours in the
panic of being overwhelmed. If all battlefield nuclear weapons were
removed, the threshold of nuclear decision-making would have
been raised to the extent that the 'use' or 'lose' dilemma would
have gone. There is a psychological advantage in NATO acting in
advance of the Warsaw Pact, or in concert, if this is the only
way forward through negotiation to remove battlefield nuclear
weapons from a corridor 150 km from the border. It would be a
demonstration, speaking louder than words, that NATO was
moving away from first use of nuclear weapons and endorsing
a no-early-use strategy. The credibility of the step would be
enhanced if it was accompanied by decisions to increase conventional armament stockpiles in Europe, to improve troop mobility
and deploy more helicopter-borne anti-tank missiles. If the nuclear
protesters were to start recommending improved conventional
armaments, their argument would be strengthened.

There is also, however, a political credibility gap that the nuclear
protesters should take into account in their attempts to produce
the initiatives that Lord Mountbatten hoped would lead 'to the
start of yet another even more vital miracle and someone somewhere will take the first step along the long stony road which will
lead us to an effective form of nuclear arms limitation, including
the banning of tactical nuclear weapons'.

Along that 'stony road' must be an understanding of the politics
of Germany, both East and West. Though divided, both governments have now powerful economies and considerable scientific
and technological know-how – both have the capacity to be
nuclear-weapon states. Neither are. The Soviets have never
allowed any other member of the Warsaw Pact to own or control
nuclear weapons. West Germany has forsworn nuclear weapons,
a decision made in the context of confidence in the US nuclear
guarantee. It is all too easy for us in the UK to talk slightingly or
uncomprehendingly about the nature of the US nuclear guarantee.
Within NATO's strategic thinking the influence of West German
political leaders is massive and inevitable. It is their perception
which rightly has the decisive influence on US policy. The Soviet

Union's acute sensitivity to West Germany developing their own strategic aircraft or long-range missiles was demonstrated by their vigorous protest following the decision of the Western European Union (WEU) in June 1984 to lift the post-war ban on West German production of such weapons. It was the first time that the Soviet Union had issued an official memorandum to the West German government since relations were normalized in 1970. It talked of acting unilaterally if necessary to stop what they see as a possible violation of the last of the remaining arms restrictions imposed on Nazi Germany at the 1945 Potsdam Conference. Soviet attitudes matter for a citizen of West Germany. They face Soviet conventional forces in all the Warsaw Pact countries across a frontier where geography favours the Soviet Union. That is why the decision to try and revive the WEU is important, for it is the forum in which the German and French bilateral security understandings can be given formal substance and provide a public affirmation of a European defence identity to offset any West German anxiety about having only the US as their defence guarantor.

The present-day policies of Europe dictate the forward defence of West Germany, for otherwise a quick conventional attack could in twenty-four hours leave the Soviet Union in control of a third of West Germany. To abandon the forward defence of Germany would be to fuel the internal movement for West Germany to withdraw or distance itself from NATO. It would also strengthen the movement to prise West Germany from NATO long fostered by the Soviet Union. That would be to usher in a new and entirely unproven political and military balance in Europe.

Some non-nuclear strategists side-step arguments over western conventional forces by saying that the Soviet Union has no intention of crossing the by now agreed East/West frontier in Europe; that the troubles in Hungary in 1956 and Czechoslovakia in 1968, and the threat of invasion to Poland in 1980–81 were within their own direct sphere of influence; that even Afghanistan was in the grey area of Soviet influence and not comparable in any way to an attack on western Europe. Honest unilateralists find such rationalizations spurious and at least argue for a strong conventional defence strategy. But few carry the logic to the extent of arguing that western European governments should pay more for a conventional defence capability. That issue has not begun to be faced, but even if it is, the non-nuclear strategists must face other problems, besides agreeing to increase the conventional defence effort. Unless they can negotiate more than just reductions in existing Warsaw Pact nuclear arms, they must argue through the implications of NATO, as distinct from Britain which raises other issues, giving up all nuclear weapons while the Soviet Union continues to maintain some nuclear-weapon systems. Despite having developed a substitute conventional holding force capable of deterring a conventional attack, they need to convince people that the Warsaw Pact would never threaten to use their nuclear weapons, even when they know that NATO had no nuclear weapons with which to retaliate. It is inconceivable, and was seen to be so by millions of people in the 1983 British General Election, that at some foreseeable date, public opinion in eastern Europe will force the Soviet Union to give up nuclear weapons; that is why it is not possible for the western democracies to abandon nuclear weapons, and with it the strategy of nuclear deterrence, unilaterally. It would certainly be better to have a conventional deterrent strategy of sufficient credibility to be in a position to be able to introduce a no-first-use nuclear strategy and to buttress this by a zone free of battlefield nuclear weapons and an agreement to reduce troop levels in the Mutual Balanced Force Reduction talks in Vienna. But for the West to abandon unilaterally the ability to threaten a second-strike nuclear response is a decision of quite awesome dimensions. To withdraw even the possibility of retaliation in the belief that no one would exploit that vulnerability goes against all past experience of how political leaders or nations actually act. Common sense rather than strategic knowledge indicates that unilateralism is a dangerous folly.

The Soviet Union is well aware of this; they have had conventional superiority since 1945, yet felt obliged to build nuclear weapons to counter the US possession of nuclear weapons. The Chinese government responded similarly, despite its large conventional forces, to the Soviets' ability to make nuclear weapons. The Pakistan government has felt obliged to build its own nuclear weapons following the Indian nuclear explosion, despite having conventional forces that have in the past held a reasonable balance when fighting India. Beleaguered Israel has developed nuclear weapons and fear of this led some Arab countries to help finance the Pakistan nuclear-weapons programme as an act of Muslim solidarity, though each country faces different threats. Countries in Asia and Latin America are at present keeping their options open by developing their nuclear weapons potential. South Africa, feeling isolated in its political laager, has developed nuclear weapons to the same point as Israel and there is considerable collusion between the two countries. The wish to retain a balance of force therefore goes deep into the nature of man and nations. There is a justified fear of accepting an imbalance in forces, for history shows that this is often the trigger for war. That is why a sense of security has to either precede or coincide with disarmament.

Political leaders, when they consider deterrence, need to give as much weight to the behavioural sciences as they do to the technological and productive sciences. It was Basil Liddell Hart, before the Second World War, who said: 'if you wish for peace, understand war', and to 'limit the danger of war, unlimited patience is needed'. The challenge for world leaders is to understand war, and not to provoke war by their impatience.

It is the neutron-bomb-deployment issue – that first triggered in 1977 the current ambivalence in the West German political leadership about NATO's nuclear strategy – that lies at the heart of the European nuclear dilemma. NATO can only move towards no-first-use of nuclear weapons at a pace which accommodates West German *angst* and West German wishes. That is not an ignoble reality – one of the central anxieties of Soviet and French political thinking concerns their fears of Germany. Reunification would represent a military threat, possession of nuclear weapons would provoke intense alarm. West Germany cannot afford to be either a conventional or a nuclear battleground. That is the reality which dictates the need for 250,000 US troops on the ground in Europe and for the British Army of the Rhine. The US Senate will not, however, put up with the European members of NATO cutting back their defence effort, and we will hear more of the 1984 Senate resolution proposing a phased withdrawal of US troops from Europe if Europe fails to improve its defence. Britain is setting a deplorable example with the government's plans to cut back defence spending in 1986 from an average of 2.8 per cent growth per year to zero growth or, more likely, an actual reduction in defence spending.

The most realistic assessment of the military balance in Europe, from the Report of the Union of Concerned Scientists, states that

while the current conventional force balance in Europe is more favourable to NATO than is commonly supposed, the US and its allies are not now in a position to adopt a no-first-use policy. Extensive consultation among the allies, culminating in substantive changes in military plans, doctrines, and decision-making procedures, would have to precede adoption of such a profound change in alliance defence policy. But the essential point is that the military improvements needed for a highly confident conventional defence of Europe are within reach and near present levels of NATO defence expenditures and manpower.

Most West Germans feel that to deter a Soviet conventional attack we need not just a strong NATO conventional force but also the possibility of US nuclear retaliation. As long as West Germany perceives any inferiority of NATO's conventional forces to the Warsaw Pact conventional forces, they will either want some US nuclear reassurance or they will seek a political accommodation with the Warsaw Pact countries. The most that West Germany can currently absorb in terms of changes in NATO strategy – and even that causes concern – is the creation of a zone or corridor free of battlefield nuclear weapons, accompanied by steps to improve conventional forces. Probably, though this is not as clear as it was five years ago, even a Social Democratic German government would want to retain the presence in Europe or its adjacent waters of some intermediate-range nuclear forces under American command.

The reason why German politicians want intermediate nuclear forces in Europe is that they do not believe that US strategic forces would be automatically invoked if a conventional war was to break out in Europe. After all it can be argued that in first Korea and then Vietnam the US has fought conventional wars and suffered 100,000 casualties without using nuclear weapons; why should the US not fight a conventional battle that meant losing Berlin and retreating beyond Frankfurt without using nuclear weapons? But German public opinion is beginning to question the value of a nuclear guarantee that could envelop them in a nuclear exchange.

For the Germans, whether the use of nuclear weapons from their territory escalates into an all-out nuclear exchange is somewhat academic. Their public debate may lead to a greater readiness than hitherto to face the lesser, though still appalling, horror of German territory being potentially a conventional battleground again. If that view prevails, and in logic it should, the challenge for NATO is to ensure that it has a stronger conventional shield in central Europe, capable not just of holding the Warsaw Pact forces but of deterring their forces from even risking a conventional war.

One of the contributions that Britain can make in achieving this conventional capability is to use money saved by the cancellation of Trident to help improve our own conventional forces.

Such a changed NATO posture would pave the way for the adoption of a strategy based on 'no early use' of nuclear weapons and the implementation of a zone free of battlefield nuclear weapons, initially in central Europe and then extending to the northern and southern flanks. Hopefully this zone would be implemented by the Warsaw Pact as well and the recently declared readiness of the Soviet Union to discuss this in the Mutual Balanced Force Reduction talks in Vienna is a useful sign.

The next step would be for NATO and the Warsaw Pact countries to give up planning and exercising on the basis of first-use nuclear strategies. If we could once stop the military daily carrying out exercises based on the belief that the politicians might authorize nuclear weapons to be used first, then sufficient trust might be achieved to move eventually to a no-first-use-of-nuclear-weapons pledge in which both NATO and Warsaw Pact countries could have confidence. In present circumstances, while nuclear weapons exist, there can be no guarantee that states possessing them would not use them if their conventional forces could not prevent defeat. There is also the danger that a pledge given in present circumstances might give rise to the belief that if a war was started, it could be guaranteed to stay non-nuclear.

The sensible course is the step-by-step approach: strengthening conventional forces; adopting a no-early-use-of-nuclear-weapons strategy; introducing a battlefield-nuclear-weapon-free zone; agreeing not to plan or exercise on the basis of a first use of nuclear weapons; removing intermediate nuclear missiles; making deep cuts in strategic weapons, retaining only second-strike strategic nuclear-weapon systems. If battlefield nuclear weapons systems and intermediate nuclear missiles were reduced drastically or removed entirely, so as to rely only on strategic missiles, which are also clearly second-strike missiles, the logical action would be to enhance that second-strike capacity. This could be done, and it has been discussed, by declaring parts of the ocean inviolate. In these areas, allocated to either the US or the Soviets and possibly China, France and Britain, there would be no military or other deployments, no surface ships would sail, no anti-submarine warfare would be conducted. The Anti-Ballistic Missile Treaty of 1972 would have to be upheld and extended to cover deployment of all anti-missile systems in space. Effectively what would then have been achieved would be a no-first-use declaration by act, not just by word. This could lead on to mutually adopting a no-first-use pledge and then, hopefully, concluding an agreement to destroy all nuclear warheads.

The Soviets will always strive for an invincible and impregnable nuclear force posture. This is a rather more accurate descriptive term of their intentions than superiority or sufficiency. There is already a gross excess of weaponry and missile negotiations are political as well as military. Above all, it needs to be remembered that we must not continue on the sterile path of nuclear account- ancy. There are political bargains to be made or at least a political deployment to be judged. Western Europe cannot allow the Soviet Union to interfere with NATO's own decision-making. The multi- lateral approach will only hold public opinion if it is seen to be boldly pursuing arms-control agreements – going beyond the knee-jerk emotionalism of nuclear-disarmament sloganizing and into the hard, painstaking nitty gritty of real negotiations. Real negotiation means calculated risks are taken, it means positions are not frozen by inertia or prejudice. Western Europe wants the process of detente to continue; it is time to demonstrate the co- operative element, which exists alongside the competitive, and to influence the Americans to exercise the political realism of restraint.

CHAPTER TEN

Enough Conservatism with a Big and Small 'C'

The British have formed the habit of praising their institutions which are sometimes inept, and of ignoring the character of their race, which is often superb. In the end they will be in danger of losing their character and being left with their institutions: a result disastrous indeed.

Lord Radcliffe, Reith Lecture, 1951

In an age in which the pace of change has quickened with every decade, in which the capacity to adjust and adapt quickly appears to be part of the process of achieving prosperity, it is not unreasonable to ask the price of the institutional conservatism that is a hallmark of British life. How much has the conservatism of government and its institutions, whether Labour or Conservative, left or right, been a factor in Britain's continued relative economic decline? Even if one concludes that conservatism has not been a dominant reason for our decline, it is hard to think that continued conservatism is a recipe for arresting the process. One does not have to believe in statism or elevate government intervention into an article of faith to believe that if Britain is to recover its economic dynamism or use its limited diplomatic clout to full effect the Whitehall/Westminster nexus of power must play a major role. Prior to the arrival of North Sea oil, it was possible to believe in a national miracle sufficient to provide of itself for our economic recovery and the restoration of our influence worldwide. But we are well on the way to dissipating the proceeds of this windfall, and providence is unlikely to provide another within the short time left for preventing our relative decline merging into absolute decline.

On the basis that Britain only embraces fundamental change when on the brink of disaster, we undoubtedly have some way to go. But the longer we delay making the adjustment and adaptation that we need if we are to prosper, the harder the task and the harsher the treatment. The fundamental change needed is simply stated: Britain has got to become more commercial, more competitive and more aware of the disciplines and opportunities in the world market in which we compete for our standard of living. It is still possible for that necessary commercial reorientation to take place, but if it is to do so, one vital element is the reform of Whitehall and Westminster. Neither the people nor the organization of Westminster and Whitehall are up to the job of reviving Britain's economic fortunes.

It is unfashionable to use the 1950s term, 'The Establishment', to describe the ruling elite. The number of civil servants who count here is less than 3,000; the circle includes MPs, leading members of the CBI and the TUC, and prestigious figures in all the professions. Turning the country round is the primary task, using that terminology in very much the same way as it is used to describe the task of putting a company back into profit or into a better trading position. Yet diagnosing the problem Britain faces in business terms does not mean that the task requires only businessmen, or the creation of 'Great Britain plc', though business attitudes and skills would not go amiss. There is no doubt that if there was the slightest chance of bringing it about, the quickest way of changing the total political configuration would be to make a change as radical as General de Gaulle did with the Fourth Republic – elect the Prime Minister directly, though retaining the monarch as head of state, while leaning further than France did towards the US system with its federal structure and explicit separation of power between the executive and the legislature. But this is wishful, escapist thinking. Britain would have to be at or on the cliff edge of economic disaster before such a radical shift could have even a chance of implementation. Our strength and our weakness is the evolutionary character of our nation.

The problem with much of the analysis of the British decline is that in rightly concentrating on economic matters, it appears not to comprehend sufficiently that economic policy making cannot be separated out from the climate and culture of the nation as a whole. One cannot pass lightly over the need to change the nature of British government at the root in order to help change British attitudes. It is attitudinal change which is so vital, organizational change is just a means – and only one of many – to an end. The call for fresh thinking is utterly right and it is typical of the establishment club that they group together so stridently to denigrate and denounce anyone who challenges their authority or experience. While there is no doubt that many outsiders, business-men or academics, by their attitudes and their training have much to contribute to improving British government, experience shows that those who are not frightened of change – whether from business, politics or the civil service – are worn down so that they either conform or get out. It is rare to stay and fight, even rarer to survive the experience. There is no evidence that businessmen survive better or longer in this atmosphere.

First and foremost, key civil servants, the ones who make the decisions and are paid reasonably high salaries, must be subject to early retirement, not on grounds of negligence or inefficiency, but for the more important and likely reason that their job could be better done by someone else. At this level of decision-making there is no room for passengers. They must have generous redundancy arrangements but we cannot go on giving the one-time brightest and best tenure even when they have become the dullest and the worst. The civil service and the diplomatic service can learn much from the up-or-out system that operates so successfully in the armed services. Indeed, security of tenure is one of the most deadening influences throughout British life. Hospital consultants, university teachers, town clerks, headmasters are all given far too great security of tenure. With the curtailment of tenure must come greater openness to new ideas and new techniques.

A Freedom of Information Act is not a luxury but an essential for ensuring that the gusts of change blow through the dust of Whitehall. No one knows about the bad decisions that are taken or who takes them. We have a vast and important decision-making structure which functions like a closed society. Under the umbrella of ineffective ministerial and parliamentary democratic scrutiny, we have an unaccountable bureaucracy that buries its mistakes. The mythology of total ministerial accountability actually mili-tates against a named individual being held to account. Account-ability must not, however, become the deadening hand that transforms government administration into a bureaucracy which dares not take a risk, where error becomes the greatest crime and inbuilt caution the recipe for advancement.

Parliament cannot go on reforming everyone else but itself; it has totally failed to retain and to exercise the power of the vote over the executive. Instead of frequent votes, monotonously and fruitlessly concentrating on trivia or party point-scoring where there is no hope of changing minds, votes should be less frequent. More often votes should be on an all-party basis dealing with specific questions aimed at the scrutiny of the executive, not on party political ritualistic nit-picking. A start could come from mandatory pre-legislative examination by select committees of all Bills, followed by an all-party committee timetabling the committee stage of all Bills. At present the nineteen Opposition Day debates are the 'property' of the Labour Party, who give, at a time of their choosing, half a day each to the SDP, Liberals and Ulster Unionists. It is a shameful abuse of democratic procedure and part of the two-party conspiracy which fixes Parliamentary procedure through the usual channels. All political parties should be allocated time for the so-called Opposition Day debates on a formula based on votes won at the last election, as with party political broadcasts. The number of Opposition Days should also be substantially increased and more Bills should have their second reading in Committee, not on the floor of the House. More debating time should be made available for short select committee debates and votes on the floor of the House. If the executive is to be better controlled by Parliament, then the creation of a '*cabinet*' around Ministers in charge of Departments should be routine; these would be composed of civil servants and outsiders appointed by the Minister, sufficient to provide a planning and thinking, as well as servicing capacity. The only way this can work and indeed the only way that Ministers can hope to influence, let alone control, their Departments is if there is an assumption that Ministers hold office for a minimum of two years. Any earlier change must be exceptional – for promotion within government or to help in the reshuffling needed to terminate a ministerial career as a result of incompetence. This will mean less movement within a Cabinet and an end to the situation which occurred recently when we had three Ministers of Transport in five months.

In addition, if Parliament and the executive are to get back any control over the bureaucracy it needs the introduction of a simple directive to apply without exception throughout Whitehall to the effect that for every new decision-making power sucked in, one decision-making power has to be given up. This will mean either terminating the power of decision or putting the decision out from Whitehall closer to the point of execution. This would avoid overload, which is one of the most stultifying factors operating within both Whitehall and Westminster, and should be accompanied by a self-denying ordinance on government legislation. The average number of clauses in Bills presented to Parliament over the past ten years could henceforth be cut by 25–50 per cent, with advantages for all future sessions of Parliament. The same arithmetical rule would also have to apply to Orders and Regulations, otherwise the machine will merely produce enabling legislation, putting all the detailed regulation into secondary legislation. Even this minimal package would have the most profound effect; without it constipation will continue to stifle the changes necessary to aid Britain's economic recovery. Neither the Conservative nor Labour Party show any sign of wanting fundamental constitutional change; that will only come from the SDP/Liberal Alliance being in a position to force change either through holding the balance of power or by forming a majority government.

When the SDP was created as a new fourth party in 1981 we talked of breaking the mould of British politics. By any standards that was an ambitious target. Despite having failed to break through in the 1983 General Election, our objective remains the recasting of Britain. We are striving for a new synthesis. We aim to be the constructive critics and the positive political force. Britain is suffering from a growing negativism, with the establishment busy buttressing the old familiar two-party conflict. Since the 1983 General Election, the SDP/Liberal Alliance has been deliberately shut out from fair and realistic coverage by the broadcasting authorities – themselves representative of the very worst of establishment thinking. The Alliance parties gained the support of 26 per cent of the electorate against Labour's 28 per cent and followed it up in the first six by-elections of this Parliament by gaining 36 per cent of the electorate's support against 33 per cent for the Conservatives and 29 per cent for Labour; even in the low poll of the European elections the Alliance received 20 per cent to

Labour's 37 per cent and Conservatives 41 per cent. No fair-minded person watching the BBC TV or ITN news programmes in the first year of this Parliament can believe that those electors who support and want to hear the Alliance's viewpoint have been given a fair treatment. Television news-reporting reflects the balance of membership in the House of Commons, not the balance of political views in the country. This carries the danger of being a self-fulfilling prophecy. During the General Election the broad-casting authorities gave a 5:5:4 split of news coverage to Conserva-tive, Labour and the Alliance, and this was broadly mirrored in the party political broadcasts. But since the election in the day-to-day news coverage it is the Labour spokesperson who is asked to comment or criticize a government decision that makes the news. Why should the broadcasting authorities be given this power to influence the future shape of British politics? There is, as yet, no way that they can be held to account, no independent assessment or judicial interpretation of fairness or natural justice. The BBC, dependent on Parliament for their licence fee, is intensely vulner-able to the old two-party conspiracy where Conservative and Labour see the Alliance as the common enemy to be squeezed out at all costs. The IBA follows the BBC; both are the creatures of political patronage, answerable to no one, elected by no one. The Alliance has had fairer coverage since the election from the daily newspapers than from the broadcasting authorities.

In the fight for fairness in television news coverage, which is the critical influence on the electorate, there are no short cuts and the Alliance parties must not fall for the belief that the only way to obtain any headlines is by cheap attacks. There is, of course, a language that is bound to be reported. There are gimmicks which one knows will get prominence. Yet one of the greatest dangers for those of us that want to change attitudes, who are aware of the complexity of modern government, who do not have strong dogmatic views and who wish to try and tackle difficult problems in a thoughtful way, is to cheapen the message. We know most arguments are won on a balance of seven to three or six to four, and that very rarely are issues so clear cut that the balance is ten to nothing. Our message, therefore, tends to be a somewhat diffuse one. We do not have emotive tunes to march to, and yet we have to get across a message of passionate moderation and commitment to the British people by the next election. They must understand why we argue for a fundamentally different approach to British politics. We must resist the ever-present danger for radical politicians of being sucked in by the establishment into the corrupting system of patronage. No Prime Minister or leader of a political party should have specific political patronage and be given as at present what is in effect a ration or allocation of knighthoods, CBEs, OBEs or MBEs for party activists. It is wrong in principle to have a separate political list; politics is as important and as honourable a profession as any other and politicians, whether local or national, should be rewarded as a normal part of an independent assessment of eligibility for honours through the Prime Minister's office.

The only area of pure party political patronage which should exist relates to the nomination of life members of the House of Lords, and even this should reflect the balance of opinion in the country and should cease when we have a reformed, representative Second Chamber with an elected element where nominated members would be chosen by an independent commission.

As far as the honours list generally is concerned, automatic knighthoods related to the job or the time served for civil servants, older MPs, ambassadors, generals, admirals and air marshals are wholly inappropriate. Nor should the House of Commons and House of Lords be seen as an extension of a London club. Both should develop further towards a functional building with the services and support to challenge, not sustain, the executive. The House of Commons should have cross benches, as in the House of Lords, and the sooner the carpenters are brought in to bridge the actual physical divide in the Chamber – along with the television cameras – the sooner the Chamber will lose its two-party, adversarial rituals. To stand out for these changes will require a good deal of courage and integrity but that is nothing to what is needed to practise a different form of politics. Instead of automatic opposition, the SDP/Liberal Alliance must be prepared to support on merit a Conservative or a Labour policy, putting forward its own distinctive viewpoint when that is dictated by objective fact, not partisan politics. The Alliance parties should be motivated by one very simple test on every issue: if something is in the country's interest, then advocate it. The jibes of 'backing Maggie' or 'letting Labour in' or being 'Thatcherite' are a small price to pay for breaking a pattern of instant opposition that is destroying the integrity and independence of British public life.

The alliance of the SDP with the Liberals is itself a wholly new political concept and controversial amongst some people even within our Alliance. It would not have been right in 1981 for some of us in Parliament to help create the SDP unless we had genuinely thought that there was a gap in British politics that needed a fourth party to express itself. Otherwise, we should have either left Parliament, which some of us were sorely tempted to do, or become Liberals. Equally, even at the point of maximum success for the SDP, at the time of the Crosby by-election, when the SDP alone was polling at the 40 per cent level, it would have been unwise to believe that we could recast British politics alone, without the Liberals. All through the early period of forging the Alliance and indeed in some senses before that in the Lib-Lab pact of 1977–8, David Steel showed courage and vision in recognizing that there was no room for electoral competition within our first-past-the-post voting system between the forces who were trying to adopt a fresh view of British politics on the radical left of centre. That is still the case; any radical rainbow must arch over our Alliance parties, embracing not just historic Labour voters but also historic Conservative voters who are showing signs of a new political awakening in the search for a radical consensus. It is an essential part of the new politics that we are trying to persuade this country to adopt that the SDP and the Liberals should demonstrate day after day, week after week, month after month, year after year, that two independent political parties can actually work together in opposition and govern together without necessarily having to merge.

If we are to persuade the British people that they should change to proportional representation (PR), it is essential to convince them that the coalitions inherent in the system will give them good government. It is not very hard to convince them of the case on fairness, for few argue that the British system of first-past-the-post voting is fair. Where the argument lies, and ought to lie, is over the nature and coherence of the coalition-type government that a changed voting system would produce. I first voted for proportional representation in Northern Ireland in 1972 and became convinced of the case for proportional representation for the 1979 European elections within a few weeks of becoming Foreign Secretary – a case which the Cabinet accepted before the Lib-Lab pact in 1977. There are few ideological factors behind my conversion, rather predominantly practical experience.

It is true that a justification of the case for PR for the European elections is that we are electing not a government, but an assembly, and therefore a representative cross-section of views is important. Certainly no one in this country should underestimate the magnitude of a change to proportional representation for elections to the Westminster Parliament. This is not a marginal minor shift in British politics, it is a major shift, and it will change the whole way in which politics is seen and the way politicians discuss and act within the British political system. Proportional representation stands or falls on whether the change will produce better government. It would not be right to advocate it on the grounds of fairness alone. Against the background of our present economic decline one could not justify such a sweeping change in our political system unless it offered the probability of better government.

It was my experience with other governments that operate a proportional system within the European Community, from the vantage point of over two years' membership of the Council of Foreign Ministers, from 1977 to 1979, that convinced me that prejudices about weak, incoherent government being associated with proportional representation were nonsense. Questions about the instability of coalition governments came up when the Dutch government took some months to form a new government after their elections. In practice, instead of there being a hiatus with no decisions from the Dutch government, the previous Ministers carried on making decisions and there was no discontinuity. I began to realize that a proportional system of elections breeds a different type of politics. The system itself builds considerable continuity within it.

Another doubt is that the continuity was so consensual that it lacked any degree of radicalism, any degree of bite or capacity to deal with controversy. Analysing the record of West Germany, the country in Europe closest in size and make up to Britain, one finds that proportional representation has produced governments which have operated with great success ever since the creation of the federal constitution after the Second World War. West Germany has prospered within the European Community, practising, with varying degrees of political emphasis, a social market economy; it has also introduced statutory support for a structure of industrial democracy. In Ostpolitik it has carried out one of the most radical foreign policies that any democratic nation has introduced in recent history. First under the grand coalition of Christian Democrats, Social Democrats and Liberals and then for thirteen years under a Social Democratic/Liberal coalition. Ostpolitik is not consensual politics – it was deeply divisive initially within West Germany, very challenging to those who wanted to cling to the United States and who feared the communism of East Germany. It was brave politics and difficult to implement, yet Ostpolitik has possibly done more for sustaining the peace of Europe than any innovation since the creation of NATO and the European Community.

Ostpolitik might not have been possible under the British political system, for even in foreign policy Britain has suffered, particularly since the 1960s, from two-party divisiveness. The opposition over British membership of the European Community is the most obvious example, with the Labour Party, the only party affiliated to the Socialist International within the European Community, being both hostile to its market orientation and its ethos of political unity. The fifteen-year struggle to defeat Ian Smith's racialism in Rhodesia was bedevilled by the difficulty of forming an all-party consensus about bringing Zimbabwe to independence under majority black rule. It is easily forgotten that Mrs Thatcher fought an election in 1979 supporting Bishop Muzorewa, only a few months before her Lusaka turnabout. The political right in the European Community countries were never able to exert such an influence on African policy and that difference is not explicable solely on the grounds of Rhodesia being more emotive for Britain because of the colonial legacy.

The left of centre in British politics ought to think very carefully before deciding that radicalism, whether in domestic or international policies, cannot flourish under a proportional voting system. While the system does not militate against change, it does make it less likely that changes will be introduced – whether industrially, economically, or politically – that do not survive the transition to a different government. Proportional representation allows for change but also encourages stability.

On the basis that politicians of the Conservative and Labour Parties can be said to have a vested interest in the status quo, and the SDP/Liberal Alliance a vested interest in reform, it is to the people that one must look for the conviction and authority to change the system, and we must not be afraid of a referendum. We have to convince the electorate not only that we should change the voting system, but that with a different system would come substantial improvements in the way we govern ourselves. It may be easier to achieve such an acceptance now that people have seen how this Conservative government has acted in the wake of its victory in 1983, overwhelming in terms of seats won despite winning less votes than in 1979, rejecting trade unionism at GCHQ or replacing the Labour GLC and Metropolitan Councils with appointed Conservative bodies is one aspect of its authoritarian, dictatorial approach; what has been done over local government rate-capping is another. Authority has been sucked in to Westminster and Whitehall, particularly during 1984, and Lord Hailsham's description of an 'elective dictatorship' looks ever closer. Centralization of power has been going on through successive governments, Labour and Conservative, ever since the First World War, and Britain is now the most deeply centralized of all democratic countries.

Giving back power to local government in a genuine way will probably only be acceptable to the electorate if they are protected against extremism, particularly the extremism of the left, which is so threatening. Only proportional representation could at one stroke so reduce the chances of extremist control in local government that it would end any possible need for rate-capping; it would also reduce criticism of the case for abolishing the rates and replacing them with a local income tax. Proportional representation also needs to be linked to a recognition, through elected Assemblies, of the nationhood of Scotland, both legislative and administrative, and the administrative and cultural nationhood of Wales and also recognition of the regional identity of some parts of England, reflected in a reformed Second Chamber. It is not necessary to dictate a single pattern of administration for local and regional government that has to be exactly the same right across the whole country. One of the characteristics of greater decentralization is a readiness to live with a degree of diversity. The

Fabianite view that greater equalization had to come from the centre has not been supported by experience. The central decisions that were going to ensure a greater measure of equality have often worked out in a way that has deepened inequalities. Instead of diversity being the enemy of equality, whether of opportunity or of provision, it has often been its friend. It is to the great credit of the Liberal Party that they were the first political party in Britain to understand the importance of decentralization as a political philosophy and principle. A commitment to decentralization is one of the important new elements that the Social Democratic Party in Britain is bringing to the tradition of social democracy. That tradition has not in the past been firmly identified with a decentralist philosophy, more often being seen as a centralist philosophy.

For the electorate not to feel misled by these changes – proportional representation, a decentralist commitment, the readiness to live with rather greater diversity – it must be admitted openly that they do represent fundamental change and, though long overdue and forming part of a logical pattern, represent a new constitutional settlement. One of the disturbing features of what is happening at the moment in the actions of the present government towards institutional reform is that one does not sense that they are part of a coherent pattern. We are seeing the mistake repeated in the 1980s under a Conservative government, that was also made through the 1960s and 1970s under a Labour government, of believing that one can play around with the constitution of this country and the government of this country in a piecemeal, partisan fashion. These issues have to be judged together and there needs to be an underlying coherent philosophy and pattern of reform against which to assess all change. Reforms cannot be introduced overnight. They will have to be phased in by consent. In their introduction there is the potential for using again the referendum first used and justified for constitutional reform over the European Community and then in Scotland and Wales. It means a legislative programme of steady constitutional reform over a ten-year parliamentary period. The reforms form part of a seamless robe running together: freedom of information, full ratification of the European Convention of Human Rights, and reform of the House of Commons. The suggested reform of the second chamber of electing under PR a regional and national element for the second chamber could be a way of giving a voice to the regions and to London deprived of the metropolitan boroughs and the GLC. The second chamber should keep some 50 per cent of nominated members chosen without political patronage to ensure the diversity of representation that can only come from people who do not want to be full-time politicians but who bring to a revising chamber expertise, knowledge and a specialism from their particular experience.

To persuade the electorate of the need to change our political system the SDP/Liberal Alliance has to win the confidence of the British people within the existing system. This was not done in 1983, for a lot of reasons, not least the aura of success that surrounded the Conservative government following the retaking of the Falkland Islands from the Argentinians in 1982. It is a blunt fact of political life that if this Conservative government's economic policies are thought to have succeeded by the time of the next election in 1987 or 1988 there will be little enthusiasm for such deep-seated political changes.

Electoral support for such substantial institutional and political changes will in the short term only be present against a background of economic and political failure. A parliamentary majority of 138 is, history shows, hard to erode in a single election if there is a background of success on the central electoral issue, namely the economy. Even what might be judged as partial success on the economy could make this government hard to beat, though it would have a substantially reduced majority. What would topple the government would be a juxtaposition of political and economic events in 1987 somewhat similar to those of 1981, with disillusionment with the Conservatives for having failed on the economy and a feeling that the Labour Party had not basically changed any of the fundamental political views on which it was decisively rejected in 1983. Such an election, whether in 1987 or 1992, will have a pretty rough political and economic background; it will be an election held against a long history of continuing economic decline, against a background where the world has woken up, or is close to waking up, to the reality that Britain's North Sea oil revenues are declining. When analysts will be able to pinpoint the moment in the 1990s when Britain will start to become a net importer of oil again. When people in Britain, as well as others abroad, will have begun to realize that we have frittered away the proceeds of North Sea oil. Against such a background Britain is going to be very tough to govern. That will be the moment of truth for the SDP, the Liberal Party and our Alliance.

The country will not vote for our Alliance if they sense at that time any weakness of purpose, indecisiveness or lack of resolve. A third-force centralist political philosophy is vulnerable to the temptation always to split the difference on every issue, even though on many issues the options are clear. The Alliance must not, however, give the impression of being just nice people, but incapable of taking determined, difficult decisions. No one can predict with certainty when the serious economic downturn will hit Britain but there is a very strong probability that it will come before the middle of the 1990s. The way the country will build up their confidence in the Alliance as an alternative government through 1985 and beyond is not so much by us telling them what we would do in government in 1988 as much as how we act facing present-day issues. They will be more likely to judge the credibility of our Alliance by how we behave over a period of time on specific, often controversial, issues, for the electorate tends to make a cumulative judgement, not to vote on the basis of manifesto promises.

The Alliance parties are therefore going to be under continuous test over the next few years. That will require a degree of self-discipline within both of our political parties so that we carry conviction with the electorate. We need, therefore, to commit ourselves to the discipline of power and the discipline of government. That means not conceding to every special vested interest or acquiescing to all expenditure demands, however worthy they are in themselves. Even the totality of new expenditure advocated in this book would probably need to be trimmed back in the light of economic circumstances at the time of an election in 1987 or 1988. We should not make commitments to unrealistic policies that we could not actually deliver in government. Behaving at all times out of government as one would behave were one in government is the discipline of being a governing party in opposition. It is very difficult to sustain. The Labour Party very rarely does so and there have often been times when the Conservative Party in opposition has been deeply irresponsible. Those two parties, however, because they have been in government before, can play around in opposition. The Alliance parties have no such luxury. We have to build up the electorate's confidence in us; demonstrate economic competence; exercise good political judgement; show soundness on defence and security issues and sensitivity to social concerns; be persuasive on the virtues of radical, political and institutional change. In addition we have to convince people on the arguments about the need for a much fairer redistribution of resources, which is not the most popular electoral political position, yet is part of the life-blood of our left-of-centre politics. There are hard choices over the allocation of capital spending and the balance of priorities for extra revenue spending. There are hard choices, too, on defence policy which turned out, much to many people's surprise, to be a key issue swinging many votes at the last election, and could well be a swing issue again in 1987–8. We will not carry credibility as an Alliance or as a government if we allow the arguments of the unilateral nuclear disarmers within our parties to make us look unsound over defence.

Radicalism is a very easy word to use and objective to aspire to. It is in practice an extremely difficult political philosophy to live up to. The best way of judging a radical is not what they say, it is how they act and what they have done. The electors hear speeches from politicians against racial prejudice, but quietly ask themselves how those politicians actually acted when under the political pressures of racial intolerance. They hear rhetorical speeches about equality and how to deal with poverty, and fairly question the politicians' own lifestyle and how they actually dealt with the issue of redistribution when they were able to make the executive judgements and decisions. What schools their children go to, what hospitals their families attend. They hear speeches about peace, but they sense that the real question is not whether the politician is in favour of peace, but how one achieves it and, once achieved, how does one maintain and sustain peace.

There are difficult dilemmas ahead for our country. We have been now for twenty years, and some would say for sixty, in relative economic and political decline, a country that still wishes that it had more power than it really has, a country which still wants, and in fact has, an influence beyond its economic and geographical weight. Yet it is a country which is still reluctant to accept the pooling of sovereignty, the wider extension of power that could come from a wholehearted commitment to the European Community and from remaining a serious partner and ally in the North Atlantic Treaty Organization. There is still within this country a degree of nationalism, insularity and self-delusion that has made it often very difficult for us to grapple in time with the necessity to take difficult decisions. There is a feeling and a fear that time is running out on this country, and yet there is a justified optimism that, despite those problems, at some time, probably fairly close to the brink, we will actually turn around and put our hands to what needs to be done and do it with good heart.

We are still divided bitterly by class. Opinion is still divided geographically between the north of the country and the south. We still harbour within our country too many prejudices, whether they are prejudices related to race, sex, or status. We need more openness, a greater capacity for self-examination. In short, we are a country with considerable problems and considerable strengths, yet we have hardly begun to face together the realities of our future, a future that must be made to work.